REAL NUMBERS

MANAGEMENT ACCOUNTING
IN A LEAN ORGANIZATION

JEAN E. CUNNINGHAM AND OREST J. FIUME
WITH EMILY ADAMS

Real Numbers:
Management Accounting in a Lean Organization

By Jean E. Cunningham and Orest J. Fiume
with Emily Adams

Managing Times Press
4400 Ben Franklin Boulevard
Durham, NC 27704
800.438.5535
© 2003 All rights reserved

Book design:
The Floating Gallery
www.thefloatinggallery.com 877.822.2500

Cover design:
IONA design
www.ionainteractive.com 919.461.9723

Illustrations:
Lisa Truitt White
HouseofDesign@mindspring.com 919.468.5616

ISBN 0-9728099-0-2
Library of Congress Control Number: 2003100419

Printed in Canada

REAL NUMBERS

CONTENTS

FOREWORD

IT IS TIME TO OPEN the kimono.

In the wake of corporate scandals that recently rocked the U.S. economy, few people still believe that secrecy in business accounting is good or desirable. After the terrorist attacks of September 11, the Dow Jones Industrial average lost not quite 7 percent of its value. In the late spring and early summer of 2002, as corporate scandals washed over the newspapers and millions of hapless investors, the Dow dropped 18 percent. The conclusion drawn by *Business Week* analysts was that tricky accounting and corporate greed did far more damage to the U.S. economy than Osama bin Laden.

A plunging stock market is just the most obvious reverberation of scandal and distrust, however. Accounting has been a mystery in most organizations since before the industrial revolution. In the beginning, it was simply good strategy to keep information on one's resources tightly guarded. As companies went public, however, and a certain openness was required, complexity took the place of secrecy. Or rather, complexity became the new secrecy. It was not long before a brilliant shell game became the rage: empty corporations could hide assets, transactions and alliances. Webs could be constructed that would require months or years of paper-chasing to unravel. As these methods became accepted practice, accountants presented an increasingly complex face to their own organizations while the entire business, likewise, became convoluted.

In a very small business, where decision-makers tend to be central and in frequent contact, this might not be a problem. But in any larger endeavor, where many people are often pulling in opposite directions toward the same goal, accurate and timely information must be a priority. That information must also be easily understood and actionable. Over the years, however, managers have been forced to understand their own departments, not in terms of income and cost, but as variances and percentages that bear little relationship to reality. Those same managers learned that variances could be nudged up or down to present a better picture of the operation—for instance, by using labor hours to make a million pieces of plastic that were not actually needed—even if that meant damaging the real business interests. Complex accounting created a kind of funhouse mirror, where the skinny man could look fat simply by shifting his position. The damage of this numbers-induced behavior is felt every day, in businesses all around the world.

What accounting should do is produce an unadulterated mirror of the business—an uncompromisable truth on which everyone can rely. It is not only investors and federal regulators that must know what lies beneath the opaque gloss of the kimono, but the management team of the business must have timely and reliable information. Only an informed team, after all, is truly capable of making intelligent decisions.

The term "opening the kimono" became widely known during the 1980s, as business people from around the world traveled to Japan to witness the industrial miracle at Toyota Motor Corporation. The term's definition is intuitive—to reveal what is hidden beneath the exterior—but few seemed to understand truly how much should be revealed. Businesses adopted just-in-time inventory systems and removed waste from their processes, but often remained blinded by old accounting practices.

In this book, Orry Fiume and Jean Cunningham present a new model for management accounting, one that will replace the 70-year-old outdated model whose primary purpose in manufacturing organizations was tracking inventory value—a purpose made moot by new lean methods. Based on the experience of transforming their own accounting functions over the past decade, the authors present a picture of a more logical kind of management accounting, one that mirrors and joins the business in its transformation. These ideas are not just relevant, but necessary. As businesses throughout the world become lean, and become more dependent on others through expanding supply chains, all economies are affected. Meaningful, timely information, presented in a way that all decision makers can understand, has become of critical importance.

Over the years, the authors also recreated their own departments on a lean model. In this book, Fiume and Cunningham offer both the big picture—why we must change—as well as useful step-by-step instructions for bringing lean into the management accounting and other administrative functions. In this way, we can see how each step of a process, and each functional department within a business, profoundly affects the next step or department.

We have all become interconnected, businesses and countries alike. Lean methodologies have changed not only individual companies, but also international trade and the economies of nations. Businesses will continue to adopt and expand upon lean because, quite simply, it makes sense to pursue a path in which we use fewer resources to create greater wealth. Now, it is time for financial managers to drop the kimono and join the rest of the business in this transformation.

Anand Sharma
President & CEO
TBM Consulting Group, Inc

1

Defining a New Role

IN TOO MANY ORGANIZATIONS, accounting teeters on the brink of irrelevancy.

Accounting departments produce information that arrives late and is often misleading. Few managers fully understand the columns of numbers and variances presented in these reports. Instead, they have learned to accept that most accounting is impenetrable. Lack of clarity, however, creates an atmosphere of distrust. That same distrust further isolates the accountant, who has become marginalized, operating behind a veil of mystery.

Is it any wonder we don't trust our financial executives? Beyond the fact that a few major corporations have used accounting's veil of complication to defraud their investors, we know that it is difficult to trust what we cannot understand.

Back in 1987, Thomas Johnson and Robert Kaplan wrote in *Relevance Lost,* "Corporate management accounting systems are inadequate for today's environment." Things have not improved substantially since then. The business world has only increased the speed and pressure.

With this in mind, consider the unlucky accountants; they studied the numbers and theories, spent money on schools to learn an honorable profession, only to be viewed as hapless bean counters—dull individuals chasing debits and credits with no better knowledge of the larger business than any other employee. They chase transactions, have heart attacks over stray invoices. This is not why they went to college.

The ingrained habits of most businesses have even reinforced the situation. The chief financial officer who tries to embrace change, using technology to handle the more mundane jobs and freeing himself to become a better business partner and advisor, often encounters resistance. Financial executives are frustrated. And their businesses are not getting what they need.

In the meantime, improvement programs have offered businesses new paths. Over the past two decades, the *lean* movement in manufacturing—emphasizing waste elimination and one-piece flow in all processes—has illustrated the potential for significant positive change. Lean, *just-in-time* or continuous improvement—all variations on the same idea—has been credited with the enormous leap in productivity that fueled the economic boom of the 1990s. Accounting, however, has largely been left in the cold. Worse yet, accounting has become a roadblock to further improvement in many cases.

There have been new ideas, new theories, to come along in accounting such as Activity-Based Costing. But ABC only added complexity to the accounting function, creating new tasks and reports instead of simplifying the process. Even now, MBA programs are filled with hopeful students who are there to "try and understand the numbers." For us, the idea that financial reports require an advanced degree to comprehend is a clear sign that change is needed.

The problem with ideas like ABC is one of narrow vision: they are based on old accounting concepts and a greater sense of the limits of accounting than real creative thought. We believe that the natural evolution of the lean movement is toward streamlining and simplicity, and that accounting systems can and should become simple and even elegant.

Drawing from the lean initiatives, we will offer methods to bring clarity to accounting, a simplicity that will help accountants move from chasing transaction to becoming true analysts and valued business partners.

Lean concepts apply to the entire organization and should be integral to accounting. In fact, we believe that accountants must become a fundamental part of the team-based improvement efforts at the core of a lean transformation. When accountants are excluded from team-based improvements, they become barriers to change because they cannot approve what they do not understand. If accountants are not involved in change, they remain mired in the old culture, along with batch processing and standard cost accounting. Once involved, however, they use their skills to help accelerate change throughout the organization.

3

We are two financial executives from the front line of the lean revolution who have found ways to lead and follow and push our organizations forward—Orry at The Wiremold Company and Jean at Lantech, Inc. We have both had extensive experience outside the financial function, in sales, retail and new product design and packaging. When change arrived at our doors, we did not see it as a threat; we saw the opportunity to eliminate elements of the accounting process that we believed were wasteful. Some financial executives are concerned that simplification will remove the mystique of accounting's "black art" and drain their power. But we did not want to be feared. We did not want to spend our days moving around data, locked away in a far corner of the business. We believed we had more to offer than incomprehensible monthly reports; we could provide the information that gives businesses a more complete picture of reality. We could be partners in change.

Some accountants that still fear change use auditors as an excuse, claiming that restrictive audits do not allow streamlining. Like Flip Wilson, they blame the auditing devil that made them do it. The auditors are not the problem. We have auditors who have accepted change that might seem radical, such as eliminating standard cost accounting systems and supplier invoices.

The walls are not so narrow as they might seem. The most difficult barriers are in our heads, and in the historical methods of accounting that have taken root in our businesses. Other obstructions are rooted in internal policy and culture rather than external rules.

We now have organizations where financial results are available as soon as the month ends, where real-time financial statements use plain English, offering data that is meaningful to business managers with no formal training in accounting. In our companies, managers can talk intelligently about the numbers, giving us the freedom to become consultants in new opportunities, rather than report-generators. And the productivity gains we have achieved in accounting have enabled us to support our growing businesses with the people we have, or without a commensurate growth in accounting staff.

We challenge executives and students alike to keep an open perspective. Do not accept the narrow view of accounting that is the conventional wisdom.

After all, belief in the conventional wisdom is what led so many into the U.S. industrial debacle of the 1970s. Content with the decades-old notion that the U.S. was the world's manufacturing giant—home of quality and efficiency—many industrialists did not notice until too late that they were getting clobbered in the marketplace. Especially in the automotive industry, giants like GM, Ford and Chrysler were losing significant market share to Japanese companies, lead by Toyota.

An NBC program that aired in 1980, "If Japan Can, Why Can't We?" was a trumpeting wake-up call that shoved the issue into the national consciousness. U.S. industrialists were forced to set aside their ideas of economic dominance and acknowledge that they had fallen behind.

Executives began taking field trips to Japanese plants, watching in awe as workers in super-clean, efficient factories put out products better and faster. Most of the executives did not know they were reversing the footsteps of one pioneering son of Toyoda, Taiichi Ohno, who had left post-World War II Japan to

5

study the ways of Henry Ford and the American supermarket system. From Ford and supermarkets, Ohno learned the value of standardization, flow, pull systems and agility. Ohno used these ideas, mixed with images from the natural world and ideas on worker empowerment, to create a system that constantly perfected itself and created enormous profitability through productivity improvements. By the time American industry was entering its most prosperous era in the 1960s, Ohno had revolutionized factories at Toyota and beyond with the ideas of continuous improvement and the *kaizen breakthrough*, which were integral to the Toyota Production System.

Those early few businesspeople studied what worked in Japan and, in many cases, adapted the processes to fit with American values such as egalitarian teamwork. In the late 1980s, the continuous improvement principles of the Toyota Production System were transforming a few early companies. But most businesses were still entrenched in batch-and-queue processes, carrying expensive inventories and trying to stave off foreign competitors through government intervention.

The tide was already beginning to slowly turn, however. In a 1990 book called *The Machine That Changed the World*, James Womack and Daniel Jones demonstrated how Toyota was able to design and build cars that consumers wanted, faster and at a lower cost than American competitors. The Toyota Production System was becoming recognized as the best and became the benchmark for world-class manufacturing.

A few years later, Womack and Jones set out to find U.S. companies that had successfully implemented the principles of the Toyota Production System. Using their own studies, plus examples from clients of Shingijutsu and TBM Consulting Group—a Japanese-U.S. collaboration that introduced many companies to kaizen early on—Womack and Jones wrote *Lean Thinking* (1996). This more clearly defined the concept of eliminating waste throughout the value chain and coined the term *lean* to describe the philosophies.

It was clear from their analysis that lean thinking applied to entire enterprises and was not intended for manufacturing alone. "As you progressively move your lean transformation beyond a physical manufacturing environment, you will find more of a need to transpose the logic of lean thinking to suit different mind-set and circumstances," Jones and Womack wrote. "Even with the most positive attitude, staff in a warehouse or a retail activity will find it very hard initially to see how flow and pull apply to their activities. After all, they don't 'make' anything in a physical sense and they've spent years blaming manufacturing for not getting its job done on time."

Two of the companies featured in *Lean Thinking*, both of which were already moving lean past the shop floor, were The Wiremold Company and Lantech, Inc. Today these two companies continue their lean journeys, consistently gaining profitability and market share in their industries. They have been transformed into companies that deliver increased value for shareholders, employees and customers.

Lantech and Wiremold customers have benefited by receiving improved customer care and a steady stream of new products designed with their input. Employees have enjoyed work that is more satisfying through greater involvement and larger financial rewards. Shareholders have received significant increases in the value of their company. Wiremold, for instance, began its lean journey valued at $30 million and skyrocketed to a value of $770 million less than 10 years later, in 2000.

If transforming a company into lean provides so many benefits, why doesn't everyone do it? Many companies try and fail. The problem is, lean principles are intellectually easy to agree with, but difficult to actually implement and sustain. It requires that we think differently, sometimes in ways opposite of our training, and that we are diligent and consistent in our actions. Also, executives must recognize that lean concepts cannot be confined to the factory. The philosophies and methods must be applied to every business process.

The underlying concept of lean is to remove waste in all forms and become a time-based competitor. Three of the underlying tenets of eliminating waste are:

- ❏ **Pull scheduling**: Make what the customer is buying right now instead of building to a long-range forecast.
- ❏ **Takt time**: The rate at which the product must be built to satisfy the customer. Change your processes so that they run only at the rate at which output is required.
- ❏ **Flow production**: Physically arrange your processes to eliminate processing things—products or transactions—in batches. Eliminate as much movement and waiting between operations as possible.

These tenets apply to all of a business' processes, including product design, manufacturing processes or administrative support processes.

There are more advantages than simple cost-savings to becoming a lean company. There are many examples of where people will pay premium price for on-time delivery of a product or service. For example, anyone can mail a letter with the U.S. Postal Service for $0.37 and feel confident that it will be delivered in two or three days with a high degree of consistency. Yet, a little company called FedEx has built a $20 billion business on the promise of delivering letters and packages the following day. People gladly pay $15 rather than $0.37 in order to gain a 24-48 hour improvement in delivery time.

FedEx could not have become the company it is without focusing closely on its process, removing waste and concentrating on that which adds value. No matter what the industry is, providing timely service that adds value to the customer is what yields results.

The Wiremold Company and Lantech are manufacturers in two very different industries. Wiremold produces wire management systems and power and data protection products. It has facilities in six countries, from the U.S. to Europe and the Far East. Lantech makes packaging machinery such as stretch wrapping machines and palletizers and has operations in both the U.S. and Europe. Although we make different products and serve different markets, we have much in common.

❑ We have adopted lean as a business strategy. We recognize that by being a time-based company, reducing the amount of time it takes to do every operation, we can increase the value we deliver to our customers and have a competitive advantage.

❑ We know that lean is not a program-of-the-month. It is an operating philosophy. Programs have an end; lean does not.

❑ We consistently use kaizen as the methodology for implementing improvement. Kaizen employs small action-oriented, cross-functional teams working within relatively tight time limits—usually between two and five days—to implement targeted improvements.

❑ We understand that lean is not just a manufacturing discipline. It is an operating philosophy that affects the entire organization. Both companies view our enterprises holistically, with every business policy and practice from sales to accounting supporting the lean philosophy. If policies or practices do not support lean, they are changed.

Over the years, both authors have had the opportunity to work with companies that are attempting to emulate our success. It has been informative to see the patterns that emerge. Most often, we see manufacturing companies being led to lean philosophies by an operations manager. Often, these managers are so intent on the excitement of transformation, they neglect their support operations, which is a bit like starting on a train trip without checking to see that all the cars are latched together. In every company that begins a lean journey without addressing its support systems, accounting becomes a barrier to transformation.

One of the nation's premiere window makers, Pella Corporation only realized in retrospect the truth of this need to latch together all support systems. Pella was first introduced to lean when three executives—representing operations, engineering and finance—attended a TBM workshop. When Mel Haught, Gene De Boef and Herb Lienenbrugger returned to Pella, they donned jeans and flannel shirts and went out to the factory floor to begin the company's lean revolution together.

"Thinking back, it was critical that the three elements were all represented at the December workshop: manufacturing, finance and engineering. I think if any one of us had come back by ourselves, we would have had a much more difficult time convincing everyone to get involved," said Mel Haught, former president and COO, now Pella's CEO.

Now 10 years into their lean journey, Pella's lead time has dropped by as much as 65 percent while sales have more than doubled. Profits are up six times; delivery performance is best in class. Finance has been a full partner throughout the transformation.

Current accounting systems were mostly developed in the early 1900s to support manufacturing products in batches. These same systems now send wrong—and sometimes disastrous—signals in a lean environment. Fortunately for Lantech and Wiremold, both companies are led by CEOs who not only allowed, but encouraged new exploration into restructuring accounting to properly report the improvements being made. We wanted to match the company-wide efforts at waste elimination. Thus, through trial and error, our idea of Lean Management Accounting evolved.

In this book you will find a few clear, repeated themes that, at this point, you may not agree with, but which we have found to be absolutely true:

❏ The CFO has the capacity to significantly add value to a company's efforts to develop and implement strategies to become world class. Accountants can and must transform themselves from focusing on transaction processing—or bean counting—to becoming valued business partners who contribute meaningful information for decision-making purposes.

❏ Financial statements, one of the major products of the accounting process, must be presented in a manner that can be read and easily understood by non-accountants. The mystique surrounding traditional financial statements can be finally excised with Plain English Management Financial Statements (Chapter 6).

❏ Accountants must change focus from Cost Accounting to Cost Management. We must abandon our obsession with developing a unit cost for each of our products, and lose the associated horrors created by standard cost accounting and its related concepts of absorption and variance analysis. Unit costs are truly only an estimate, given the number of subjective allocations that go into the sum, and often lead to poor decisions. Understanding costs at a higher level and providing tools to manage them better should be our real goal.

❏ Mind what you measure. To paraphrase an old saying, *you are what you measure.* All companies attempt to establish metrics to determine if they are achieving their goals. Unfortunately, many of these measures are too complex for the average worker to be actionable, and some create dysfunctional behavior.

❏ All accounting systems contain waste. As with any other business process, accounting processes can be improved to eliminate waste and allow for more time-ly reporting of valuable information.

❏ The annual budget process for most companies is approached with dread and sometimes, derision. Budgets, however, can be *meaningful*.

❏ Understanding lean and how it applies to the entire organization gives a company superior advantage in the world of mergers and acquisitions. By being able to see lean opportunities in target companies, the lean buyer is in a position to outmaneuver companies interested in the same target. The lean buyer does this by recognizing that it can pay a higher premium to the seller while still decreasing the payback period for its investment.

If all this sounds like alchemy, be assured it is not. It is hard work. In the following pages, you will find concrete examples of actions we took—with the help of many people in our organizations—to achieve these results. We believe that this book will be helpful to the CEO, CFO, and all leaders of those companies that have embarked on the lean journey. Even if a company has not chosen this route, we believe that a CFO can make use of many elements within lean management accounting to better his processes.

When introducing these concepts to the skeptical, one of the objections we often hear is that of scalability. "My company is smaller than yours and lacks the resources, so we couldn't possibly do this." We hear, "My company is much bigger than yours and our complexity prohibits this sort of thing."

But we have seen that these principles can be successfully implemented in any company—whether it is manufacturing or service-related—of any size. A smaller company *needs* to do this because its resources are limited and the hidden waste hinders them. Large companies *need* to do this because size has introduced unnecessary complexity that must be eliminated before a more agile competitor steals its business.

In all companies small, medium and large, adopting lean as a business strategy has significant benefits for the customers, for employees and shareholders. Lean manufacturing is not enough. Lean engineering, lean marketing and distribution and purchasing and lean accounting must be implemented if we are to embrace future success.

The journey is long, but the rewards are many.

2

FROM BEAN COUNTER TO
BUSINESS PARTNER

WHEN A STUDENT OF FRENCH WORKS TOWARD a college degree, it is not with the goal of simply speaking French. True, they should be able to speak the language, but the real purpose is to teach or translate, or maybe enter the field of international relations. Likewise, the goal of an accounting education is not to prepare for a lifetime of recording debits and credits, but to learn a language and tools to assist a business toward better performance.

So, we go to school for four years or more to learn accounting techniques and we figure, if universities offer graduate studies in Accounting, surely it cannot be simple. With this in mind, we focus on complexities such as process accounting, consolidation and FASB pronouncements and end up learning and using an entirely separate language. We don't talk about how many widgets we need to make; we talk about volume variances. That language separates us from our colleagues in operations, sales and other business functions. Because we're not using simple, plain language, the gap is widened further.

We accountants are not the only ones creating a protective niche with language and concepts. Engineers, lawyers and IT professionals all create and then protect their own slang. Together, we have created something like a Tower of Babel; with accountants doing a particularly good job laying the bricks of obfuscation. Before we add to the general miscomprehension, we should clearly explain a few of our terms.

There is a difference between bookkeepers, accountants and financial analysts. Bookkeepers record transactions such as bill payment and money collection. These are clerical positions, usually accomplished without a college degree. Accountants might spend a certain amount of time bookkeeping, but they are also responsible for producing financial statements and some of the other more demanding aspects of accounting. Some accountants specialize in taxes or acquisitions. Finally, the financial analyst interprets information—such as analyzing the return-on-investment of a particular machine or calculating company valuation. There are different ways to look at the work or to break down work responsibilities, but as a group, these are the people responsible for providing all the financial information and activities a company requires. In this book, all of these positions will be referred to collectively as accountants.

Our goal is to break down the walls between these separate activities, and then break down the walls between accounting and the rest of the organization. We see too many accountants on the sidelines when they are needed as an integral part of the organization. If you work in an accounting department, look at where your department is and where people go during the day. Do the accountants come in, sit at their desk and remain fixed there all day long? Are they far from the rest of the action? Do they ever go to the site where parts are being purchased, where products are being designed? If they do not, if people from throughout the business have to come to accounting to seek information, it is a good indication that the accounting team is sidelined. We cannot remain immobile and hope to be a vital part of the business.

Changing the financial function, even radically, is not a new concept. The Financial Executives Research Foundation (FERF) has been publishing studies on this subject for years. "Finance people can be more effective by getting to know the business and helping their manufacturing and marketing colleagues make better decisions, instead of being functional stars concerned with purely financial matters," one study stated.[1]

"Finance people have sometimes suffered under the image of 'naysayers' and 'bean counters' that were primarily concerned with control and budget variances.

"The emphasis of financial practice is shifting away from control and more towards business advocacy and providing value-added services."

The following year, another study found that, "true reengineering demands a radical rethinking of everything that is done in finance. The challenge is not simply to 'tweak' and 'tinker' with

---

1 "The Empowered Organization: Redefining the Roles and Practices of Finance" Financial Executives Research Foundation, 1994.

functional processes. Reengineering requires focusing on structural change and looking at the various activities within finance from a broader, cross-functional perspective. The vision is one of driving down transaction processing costs, redirecting the flow of work toward more valuable kinds of analysis, and earning for the finance staff an expanded role in strategic decision making."[2]

These studies were published in 1994 and 1995, respectively. Still, the message seemed lost. In a 1998 follow-up, "Changing Roles of Financial Management: Integrating Strategy, Control, and Accountability," the authors found that financial executives see themselves in a more positive light than their non-financial peers:

"In follow-up discussions with executives and managers (especially non-financial managers) at other firms...many of these managers indicated that the command-and-control and conformance orientations were alive and well within their firms. This feedback led us to wonder if a 'rhetoric/reality' gap might exist between the perceptions of financial managers and non-financial managers."

This study included the results of a survey of non-financial managers, in which only 32 percent believed that their financial people were actually involved in the business and just 11 percent believed that their financial people were responsible for integrating business operations.

However, 29 percent believed that their financial people were in place for "oversight and surveillance purposes." Another 27 percent thought financial people "exist to enforce compliance with the firm's policies and procedures."

---

2 "Reengineering the Finance Function," Financial Executives Research Foundation, 1995.

Which makes accountants something like the business police.

A recent survey by Robert Half International, Inc., one of the largest staffing firms specializing in accounting and finance personnel, entitled "The Next Generation Accountant" stated that "...today's CFOs say they expect nontraditional accounting functions to occupy 37 percent of a senior accountant's time in five years..." It also stated, "An increasing corporate reliance on cross-functional teams is creating the need for cross-functional professionals...In addition to a firm grasp of marketing and operations, accounting and financial professionals must recognize the impact of financial data on the business as a whole and on individual departments."

Meantime, our colleagues in operations have been closer to the cutting edge. Over the past decade, the U.S. economy has benefited from big productivity gains in the manufacturing and, to some degree, service sectors. In his comments regarding a 2001 rate cut, Alan Greenspan referenced the dramatic reductions in stock and inventory manufacturers had achieved in prior months. With less inventory and quicker reaction times, Greenspan pointed out, manufacturers had responded very quickly to the fluctuation in demand and we all felt the economic slowdown in real time. The e-commerce influence is driving many businesses to house smaller quantities and make more frequent shipments, even if they do not understand lean. The demands on business have been tremendous and U.S. manufacturers have been meeting the challenge. But like an island in the stream, the accounting areas have remained rooted to the methods that have been taught in business schools for decades.

When Jean attended business school to receive her MBA, she was in a program with managers who all had 10-20 years of business experience. These were all successful business people, but when they were asked on the first day why they were pursuing an MBA, more than one third answered, "So I can understand the numbers." This was preposterous, and a little disheartening. Jean had an undergraduate degree in accounting, so her goal on entering an MBA program was to learn how to lead, motivate and strategize. To earn an MBA, she believed, meant you were preparing to be a leader in your field, with a focus on learning to evaluate competitive challenges for your company, to learn national and international management techniques and to develop long-range strategies. But one third of her fellow students said they needed an advanced business degree to learn to understand the numbers that accountants generated.

This signaled a serious problem in the finance and accounting functions. Basic information—the numbers of a business—is very simple. It is all about adding, subtracting, percentages and ratios—skills that are taught in grade school. Yet, when Jean gave it some more thought, it began to make sense. People feel they have to learn "the numbers" because we throw around terms like *ROI, margins, variances, turnover, utilization, ROA* and *DSO* like a complex code. This is what keeps us separated from the rest of the organization.

Consider the organizations that have gone to open-book management—a move that companies make in order to promote trust and a sense of personal ownership in the business. It's a big step in most companies, to commit to this kind of openness, and the roadblocks are more numerous than one might envision. Imagine trying to throw open books that are written in code. It is doubtful that management would be trusting and employees would feel more committed to the company's success when confronted with impenetrable code.

Some businesses have gone the route of teaching all the people in a business how to understand the numbers. We have seen companies create two- and three-day classes for everyone in the organization—every single associate—to help them understand the numbers. In effect, they are trying to provide the Rosetta stone of accounting. The American Management Association has a course called Accounting for Non-Financial Managers that appears to be wildly successful, where students study for an entire week just to receive the keys to the financial reports.

Wouldn't it be easier to make the numbers understandable? Shouldn't we use the tools and language that people already understand like adding, subtracting and percentages? Change the reports, not the people. (In the chapters on Performance Measurements and Plain-English Management Financial Statements, you will find some great tools to break down accounting codes into easily digestible statements.)

At Lantech, there would be monthly business group meetings at the cafeteria. Shop floor guys in their coveralls would slouch into chairs; a few executives would stand around the edge, clutching coffee in disposable cups. Someone would welcome new employees and then give Jean her cue: "Let's talk about the numbers."

Jean would put up her overhead slides and explain that last month they shipped more than the month before. A few people would be nodding. Then she would start to explain the profit variances. The standard for the product was less than it actually took to build, Jean would explain, and materials variances were a little lower because the vendor charged less. At this point, Jean would usually glance around the room to see if anybody has a clue of what she was talking about. Sometimes she wasn't sure she understood either. There would be no questions from the small audience; nobody looked like they were paying any attention at all. So, Jean would drop down to profits and show that profit had dropped from the month before even though more product was shipped. Now there might be a few people shifting uneasily in their seats, but still no comments. On those months, Jean expected more profit to be shown and everyone else probably did too, but nobody said anything. They had seen others ask the question before and knew already that the answer was nothing to which they could relate. And Jean was forced by time constraints to give little more than superficial answers.

At Lantech these days, no financial person needs to be at hand to present the numbers—anyone can do it—and the whole company comes to the cafeteria to participate. There are colored graphic slides that show the level of shipments and someone will make specific comments about product lines—which one is selling—and focus on new demand. Then the presenter can say, "As go shipments, so go profits." If there is not a direct correlation, there is a clear reason. Someone might say, "This month we had lower profits because we had a large trade show and a lot of people had to travel." People ask questions about the quality of a particular product, or ask questions about warranty returns. Finally, everyone understands that cost is a function of quality.

From this description alone, it is clear how Jean changed her position within the company. Once an outsider with highly segmented information, also known as a traditional accountant, she is now a business partner. No longer chained to her desk, Jean and her team know they belong in the purchasing area, on the shop floor, in the accounting department—anywhere they can provide information. Jean concentrates more on providing help with decisions about product pricing, investments and hiring, on pulling the numbers together to help clarify choices.

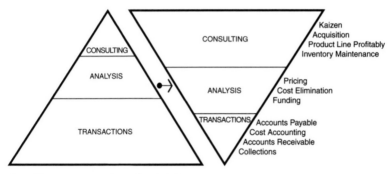

Figure 2.1 Accounting and Finance Transformation

So maybe this sounds like a great idea, but where does one begin to change? First, take a good look at the people in the accounting area. What are they doing right now? The triangle in the above illustration (Figure 2.1) is a simple way to describe the work content in an accounting team. In the largest part of the first triangle are the ubiquitous transactions. Probably two-thirds of the people in most accounting departments are working on transactions: paying bills, collecting money, filing taxes and paying people. Then there are a few cost accountants, fixed-asset accountants and someone responsible for creating the financial statements. There might be a couple of financial analysts checking to see how much is being spent and evaluating capital investments. Finally, there is probably a controller or CFO who goes to the business planning meetings and works on the budget and planning. We'll refer to that last category as consultants or business partners. If the area in the triangle represents time spent, the base of the first triangle shows that the largest amount of total time is spent in transactions.

Then we need to ask, what does the business need from us? What does the CEO value enough to pay our salaries? Unfortunately, those CEOs probably want help understanding the numbers. But they also need our help growing the business profitably. The CEO wants help finding the resources to fund a new project; she wants to know where we can improve costs in products and services, and she wants to know whether improvements made have resulted in financial gain. The CEO needs help seeing where the company has improved or declined and what the future looks like given the current circumstances. The CEO asks, "What are my choices?" Answers to these questions are worth good money.

On the other hand, what are most businesses paying for now? Sure, the bills need to be dealt with, money collected and people paid. Taxes must be paid to keep us all out of jail. But the first triangle must be turned upside down without necessarily adding new staff. At Lantech, there was the same number of accountants in 2001 as in 1991, even after doubling the business.

To get to the point where Lantech could double the business without doubling the accounting department, and have accounting become more relevant, the office needed to be overhauled. The newly lean accountant will need to exert all the leadership qualities he or she has in order to overcome resistance. This is not a duty that can be delegated; leaders must create the vision that will overcome constraints. It's hard to take a chance and change a well-established routine. Everyone has relied on these time-honored approaches for a very long time. This book should give you confidence, however, in knowing that there are others who are finding ways to change.

As a preview, here are a few things the finance and accounting leader will hear as you struggle toward change:

> *We have always done it that way.*
> *This is what the contract says.*
> *Our auditors told us to do that.*
> *I need those files.*
> *We will lose control if we eliminate that.*
> *That's too risky.*
> *We need the hard copy.*
> *I need those files.*
> *I won't do anything outside of GAAP.*
> *I need to know the exact cost of that item.*
> *That isn't the right answer.*
> *I need those files.*

Overcoming resistance to change is often very time consuming, so be prepared. The leader of change must take the time to talk, ask questions, probe further. We need to ask: "Why do you need that? What happens with that information?" This should not be a shaming experience for the employee; this must be a learning experience for the leader if we are to find the best path to proceed. Listen with an ear toward moving forward with the new information you are gathering, not stopping the journey.

In accounts payable at Lantech, for instance, we would pay the bills for the week and then sort the bills alphabetically by vendor name, carefully putting them away in the proper vendor folder.

It was a time consuming activity and it wasn't clear that it was adding any value. When Jean suggested change, however, the initial reaction was, "We have to do it that way. When Acme calls to see if I've paid the bill, I can go to that folder directly and answer."

The next question might be: How often does that happen? In Lantech's case, the answer was that Acme calls maybe once every three months. When they did call, it took no time to look up, but the actual collating and filing was time consuming indeed.

How about if, instead, we just file the invoices by the date they were paid? When the vendor calls with a question, a clerk can look on the accounts payable system to see what day the bill was paid, then search the file containing bills for that particular payment date. It would take longer to find the specific bill and answer the question, but less time than it took to alphabetize and file every bill, every week. At Walker Systems, a subsidiary of Wiremold, adopting this method saved an entire man-year of work. That is a small example of timesavings, but the real point is listening to your people. When people know they will be listened to, that their concerns will be acknowledged and we will look for logical conclusions to make everyone's work easier, they will be more willing to be open to new solutions. In this case, leadership is listening and making sure that accountants feel they are part of the solution.

One refrain a CFO is likely to hear in a transformation is, "The system makes me do it that way." This one is a particular favorite. Lantech used to keep books of all the sales invoices sent out, organized by month and order number. There were cabinets full of these books lining the walls, pushing into open areas and used as space dividers. "We need hard copies of every invoice," accountants told Jean, "in case we have to look it up." It was the system.

Jean gently pointed out that all the same information was available on computers. "Wait," the accountants said, "what if I need to fax a copy of the invoice to the customer?" That's a valid point; it does happen occasionally. Of course, the clerk could just print it out only when asked and then fax it to the customer, thereby saving all of the copying, printing and filing motions for every single invoice. Taking it a step further, Lantech eventually purchased fax software so anyone could fax directly from a personal computer. No paper involved.

Lantech sold those cabinets that used to hold the books, and now the accounting team has more space to move around than any area at Lantech—even after moving the information-technology staff into accounting. This is the kind of hands-on leadership that will be required to make the change to lean accounting.

Make no mistake: there will be barriers. Once a company dramatically lowers inventory, the financial statements will get confusing, especially if standard cost and variance-style income statements are still used. The cost from the old inventory must be included in the expense column. The result will be opposite of what most organizations would expect. For a time, profits will look lower and the results will look worse from doing the right thing (see example in Figure 2.2). Just remember, the real expense of carrying inventory was hidden under the old system. (You will get hints on how to deal with this in Chapter 6.) That's one more barrier to advancing toward lean management accounting.

	Batching	Lean
Beginning material at cost	5,000,000	5,000,000
New purchases	+ 2,500,000	1,250,000
Ending material at cost	Ð 5,000,000	3,750,000
Material cost	= 2,500,000	2,500,000
Labor cost	+ 750,000	750,000
Overhead costs	+ 1,000,000	1,000,000
Actual or lean costs	= 4,250,000	4,250,000
Deferred labor and overhead		
from inventory reduction	+ 0	612,500
Cost of goods sold	= 4,250,000	4,862,500
Income Statement:		
Sales	4,500,000	4,500,000
Cost of goods sold	Ð 4,250,000	4,862,500
Gross Profit	= 250,000	Ð362,500

Unfavorable profit from inventory reduction; but this is just showing costs the accounting system allowed you to wait to expense until product sold.

	Batching	Lean
Cash position is		
dramatically improved:		
Purchase inventory	2,500,000	1,250,000
Labor cost	+ 750,000	750,000
Overhead cost	+ 1,000,000	1,000,000
Total cash used:	= 4,250,000	3,000,000

Cash is improved by 30% or $1,250,000

Figure 2.2 This Company Reduced Inventory by 25% and Increased Cash by 30%

The pressure to make the month is another barrier. For public companies, there is terrific pressure to meet the projected numbers every quarter. Even the smallest reduction in your earning, compared to projections or prior quarter results, can mean a death toll for the stock price. Sometimes, it means the job of the CFO. And this is not just a problem for public companies. Often there are bonus programs tied to profits or sales, or bank loans tied to results or inventory balances. These are real issues and must be considered, not as a roadblock but as a factor to include as you make necessary improvements. There is no single magic answer to show public companies how to deal with this issue. One public company that implemented lean made huge reductions in inventory and was forced to recognize the high cost of old inventory, which reduced reported profit. They worked closely with the Wall Street analyst that covered their company, however, and were able to show the real cash flows and business benefits of reduced inventories through lean practices. This way, the analyst could understand the positive future implications of the current events.

As you work through the barriers, take courage from knowing that many obstructions are of our own making. Over time, you have become locked in certain measures and those same measures have very likely become improvement barriers for other departments. Consider accounting's complicated ways of figuring the worth of a machine, for instance. Our measures—our rows of logical numbers—keep a piece of equipment constantly utilized. Accounting said this machine must be run constantly to make it profitable, keep unit cost low and keep from having unfavorable variances. So the company buys materials it doesn't need, pays an operator to run parts that are not needed and puts unnecessary wear and tear on the machine. This is all done because accounting blessed the machine's purchase based on specific parameters, which included sales projections that were too optimistic. Now we say, if you don't need the parts, don't run the machine. We need a new mindset regarding idle time.

All barriers aside, we do acknowledge that there are good guidelines, or retaining walls, that accountants depend on. Be assured that nothing in Lean Management Accounting violates GAAP (Generally Accepted Accounting Principles). Pick up any beginning accounting textbook and you will find the four basic tenets of accounting:

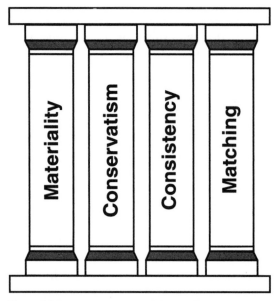

Figure 2.3 The Four Columns of Accounting

Materiality

This is one of the tenets most misunderstood by modern accountants. The concept is simple but applying it on a daily basis is not. The official version issued by the Financial Accounting Standards Board states:

"Materiality is a pervasive concept that relates to qualitative characteristics, especially relevance and reliability. Materiality and relevance are both defined in terms of what influences or makes a difference to a decision maker, but the two terms can be distinguished. A decision not to disclose certain information may be made, say, because investors have no need for that kind of information (it is not relevant) or because the amounts involved are too small to make a difference (they are not material). Magnitude by itself, without regard to the nature of the item and the circumstances in which the

*judgment has to be made, will not generally be a sufficient basis for
a materiality judgment. The Board's present position is that no general standards of materiality can be formulated to take into account
all the considerations that enter into an experienced human judgment. Quantitative materiality criteria may be given by the Board
in specific standards in the future, as appropriate."*

In addition, the Securities and Exchange Commission (SEC)
offered this opinion:

"Exclusive reliance on certain quantitative benchmarks to assess
materiality in preparing financial statements and performing
audits of those financial statements is inappropriate; misstate-
ments are not immaterial simply because they fall beneath a
numerical threshold." [3]

The bulletin then discusses at length the circumstances under
which a misstatement may be considered material, with specific
focus on decisions made by the investment community. It states
in part, "A matter is 'material' if there is substantial likelihood that
a reasonable person would consider it important." The Supreme
Court has also addressed this subject, with similar results.

Thus we do not want to underestimate the complexity
involved in making decisions about materiality, especially
when publicly issued financial statements are involved, but will
address the issue from an internal standpoint. This is information that management is using to make daily decisions about
the business.

---

3 Securities and Exchange Commission, Staff Accounting Bulletin No. 99:
  Materiality released in August 1999.

Put another way, Materiality is where precision and accuracy get confused. Precision is knowing the answer down to the third decimal point. Accuracy is the answer that is correct for the decision you're trying to make. A good example of this is gas mileage. When you bought your car, mileage was probably part of the equation. If the dealer's sticker promised 22 miles per gallon, you probably expected between 20 and 24. To get an accurate portrayal of your real gas mileage over time, you would record your miles traveled and divide that number by the gallons of gas you bought. This gives you an accurate picture. Precision is when you hire an accountant to ride in your car with you and calculate down to the third decimal that you get 23.947 miles to the gallon on this trip, 24.237 on the next, etc.

When defining materiality, ask if you would change the business decision you're about to make if you knew the answer to the question within plus or minus 1 percent, 5 percent, or 10 percent? This will tell you the materiality threshold for that issue, and where the borderline is between precision and accuracy.

Conservatism

In plain language, this means that you should not over-emphasize the good news or under-emphasize the bad news. Anticipate your losses but not your gains.

Warranty reserves are based in conservatism. In a practical sense, conservatism tells us to record all possible expenses immediately and wait to recognize revenue until the last reasonable moment. Pressure to show positive results in the organization can be very strong. One of the most important ethics the accountant brings to the table is the insistence on conservatism that will keep companies out of trouble. This doesn't mean, of course, that all companies abide by conservatism.

Although in relative terms the percentage of publicly owned companies that have restated earnings since 1995 is small, there has been a dramatic increase over the past three years. From 1998 to 2000, there were 464 financial restatements.[4] This total was higher than that of the previous ten years combined. According to the study, the most common reason for restatement was revenue recognition.

In the year 2000, revenue recognition was the cause of eight of the top ten restatements, measured in terms of market value loss. The study concluded that one of the factors driving the increase was the "higher performance pressure on management teams" to achieve dramatically higher equity returns. In a Wall Street Journal article about the study, Philip Livingston, president and CEO of Financial Executives International said the pressure "pushed some management teams to stretch accounting rules to the breaking point, ultimately prompting restatements." Even though the FERF study concludes that because the number of restatements is small, and therefore "the overall quality of financial reporting is high," the increasing trend is troublesome. Since this study was published the number and magnitude of restatements has become such a significant issue that it has rocked our financial markets and prompted new legislation. This is shameful, and an indication that the companies' last line of defense, the chief financial officer, was not able to withstand the pressure and agreed to break the rules.

---

4 From a June 2001 study of earnings restatements published by the Financial Executives Research Foundation.

Consistency

Consistency guides us to present facts in the same manner each time they occur. By presenting or reporting them consistently, the trends presented over time will have meaning because they are based on a common method of presenting similar facts. It is all about providing information that is helpful to interpret the situation.

The best way to understand something is to learn it, and then be able to rely on it being the same each time you look at it. If you always put your toothpaste in the same place after you use it, you can rely on its placement. Might there be another place to put it? Sure, but knowing it is in the same place makes your routine easier. As a practical example, if you record freight as a product cost, consistency says you should keep reporting it that way, in the same account and location every time. If you make it a reduction to sales one month, then move it down to product cost the next, the information about whether sales are up or down is confusing and unreliable. Once the accounting information becomes hard to rely on or understand, the accountant has lost his value to the organization.

Consistency seems to say, "Don't change." This book, on the other hand, is advocating change. So how do we justify this? Remember the goal: providing useful information to business managers. Consistency will help you do this, but only if the consistent information is useful in the first place. If you do change formats or methods, remember to disclose it when appropriate, or restate prior results consistent with the new method to help users understand the figures.

Matching

All costs to manufacture the goods you sell must be recognized as an expense in the month you recognize revenue. Most costs need to be recognized in the month they happen. A practical example: the materials that you bought for a product that will ship in two months will be kept as inventory on your balance sheet. It is not an expense until you ship the product. The cost of advertising that product, or any other, is recorded as an expense on the books in the month it happens. This was the genesis of a lot of standard cost accounting techniques.

This is an important tenet from a lean manufacturing perspective because, as lead times shrink on products that are being made and shipped all in the same month, there is an opportunity to simplify accounting procedures. When products are made and shipped in the same time frame, accountants no longer need to put the manufacturing costs of people and overhead on the balance sheet as inventory. We can expense these costs directly as they occur and still match our expenses with our revenue. At Lantech, the elimination of standard cost absorption alone released one of eight accountants to begin doing other things—notably, analysis work on overall product line profitability.

ONE OF THE MOST IMPORTANT retaining walls for accounting's structure is not a traditional accounting tenet. If it were, the tenet would be called the company's mission or objective. What the company is trying to achieve should be our guideline for determining what we report and what we measure. After all, we want to be in the stream moving with the business, giving information that is relevant instead of paddling against the current or jumping out of the water.

For instance, perhaps your company's competitive advantage is introducing new products rapidly. Information about development time to market and tracking the related cost to enhance tax incentives might be critical. Accounting should consider it a priority to have precise records of this information. Perhaps in your business, the cost of oil is one of the most critical factors, or you rely on government contracts, with pricing based on cost. Then these factors must be taken into consideration when developing the right kinds of techniques for your accounting reports in order to help ensure that the company meets or exceeds its goals.

For Lantech, one of the most important pieces of information needed was product line profitability. Management wanted to know how competitive pricing could be, while maintaining acceptable profit levels for each product family. So accounting focused on evaluating the amount of resources it took to build a complete product family. The business focus told accounting there was no need to ascertain the cost of each individual product. The cost of individual units is not tracked and not compared, month to month. Managers need to know cost and sales trends; they also wanted to know the value of what was spent on trade shows. Accounting decided to track cost per lead, from trade shows or advertising, and the number of orders for a type of machine and how many shipped. The company's objectives were the guide. Knowing the objectives, accounting could customize reporting in order to remain relevant. Reports could now reflect whether projects were moving in the right direction.

The core tenet of Lean Management Accounting is a basic assumption that everyone in accounting would rather be a valued partner in the business rather than a bean counter. To become an asset, we must stop drowning in the sea of our own transactions. Grab a life raft and see where the journey leads.

3

PERFORMANCE MEASUREMENT

To know the true picture of a company, to ascertain whether it is improving or slipping down the wrong path, we know we must collect and keep certain performance measurements. Also, we know there should be one driving force behind which measures are selected and *deselected*: the company's strategy and related goals.

Look at it this way: If performance measures are to create an accurate picture of the company on which we can rely, then the strategy is the tool we use to guide our focus, like operating a camera. Selecting goals and measures is like building a strategy camera. Every camera takes a slightly different picture; build one badly, and the output will be shadows and distortion.

The first and most important consideration for the lean accountant and executive is to ensure that the goals identified are critical to success. Experience teaches us that when goals are set, people will do whatever they can to achieve the target, even if it results in dysfunctional behavior. Consider the craze of the 1970s and 80s, MBO or Managing By Objective. All that focus on the *what* part of the equation—the objective—instead of the methods for achieving the objective created loopholes that hurt a lot of businesses. In the end, MBO often created suboptimization, with managers eagerly optimizing the one little piece of the process over which they had control, without concern for the big picture. It is a kind of natural law that people will try to meet the metrics set by the boss in order to make themselves look good, no matter the consequences.

We know that metrics shape behavior. So we need to look for the metrics that will result in the desired behavior, and be certain that we are establishing measures that managers and associates can relate to their specific jobs. Metrics can be long-term in nature or can be created to address a more immediate, short-term problem. For instance, if energy prices spike, a metric can be created to focus employee attention on that issue for the length of time that it remains an issue.

In one light, performance measures can be viewed as a simple roll-up of the business' mathematics. Once a team begins to explore the many levels of the equation, however, some people might get lost—unable to see how to get to the bottom line when there are so many layers in between. We should be able to clear up much of that confusion in this chapter.

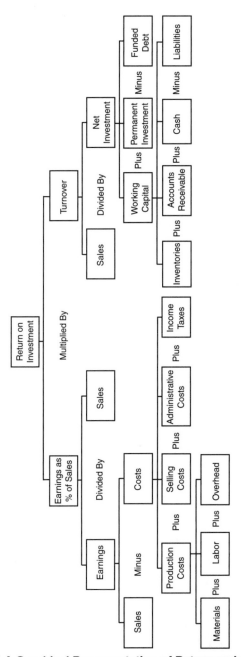

Figure 3.1 A Graphical Representation of Return on Investment

One of the business world's premier measures, stressed in most financial management programs and treated as the one prevailing metric, is Return on Investment or ROI. As currently practiced, ROI is an excellent example of the intent to capture many complex and interrelated events, thus creating one monster of a metric that few people can relate to their daily activities. Figure 3.1 demonstrates the complexity of this measurement. This type of illustration is rarely, if ever, used to help employees understand how they can relate to ROI. As we can see, however, most people can affect an ROI metric at a point that is five or six levels deep. But most employees believe that ROI is some esoteric financial concept that doesn't touch them in their daily lives.

The reality is that ROI is merely the complex reflection of all the activities of every individual on every day of the period being measured. In other words, ROI is the attempt to encompass everything in one number. It becomes clear that if we focus on measuring improvements in how people work—in bettering the process for each piece of work—those improvements will roll up into an improved ROI.

Employees can more easily relate to processes, since every person uses some type of process every day. So we focus on improving the process by highlighting performance measures that are focused and less all-encompassing than the final ROI. If a company is constantly improving its processes, the results in the ROI will come. This focus on improving the individual elements of the process, by eliminating waste and increasing velocity, has great impact on the bottom line, but only when we are not focused exclusively on that bottom line. The winners will be companies that focus on process first, not results.

The question now becomes, which process performance measurements should be kept and which deselected? Art Byrne,

Wiremold's CEO, says if he were forced to use just two metrics for the entire company, he would choose customer service and inventory turns. Byrne explains it this way: a company cannot have high customer service—which might be measured in part by the percentage of on-time delivery—and high inventory turns without doing a lot of things right. High inventory turns means the business has achieved high velocity and eliminated significant waste throughout the organization.

Compare these simple measures with the one big hammer of a metric many companies use: Make The Month. There are businesses that expend tremendous amounts of energy and resources toward the end of the month in one mad scramble to live up to whatever numbers were budgeted or promised. Make-the-month might seem like a rather simple trap to avoid, but most typical results-oriented companies end up in the make-the-month category. These businesses may get results in the short term—much as fad diets get results—but in most cases, the practice creates significant waste that can seriously damage a company in the long term. How can we tell if a company has fallen into this trap? If we use the example of shipments, look at whether shipments reflect substantially more than 25 percent of monthly sales in the last week of a typical four-week month. If the answer is yes, make-the-month syndrome is at play. We have seen companies that regularly ship 50 percent to 80 percent of their monthly volume in the last week of the month. The resource implications of this are staggering. What are the resources, such as overtime, that are needed to process 80 percent of the volume in 25 percent of the time? Or, if the organization has staffed to comfortably handle that higher volume, then what amount of resources is sitting idle or involved in make-work activities the other 75 percent of the time?

When Art Byrne joined Wiremold in 1991, the first slide of the first presentation that he made to employees was this:

Productivity = Wealth

Although simple in its form, this statement expresses a key economic principle. In fact, it is this principle that has been an essential element of Alan Greenspan's campaign to fight inflation. Productivity gains allow companies to increase wages without increasing prices. This in turn keeps inflation below the wage-increase level, thereby increasing real income and the standard of living. However, productivity is a much-misunderstood concept and often misused. Simply reading a company's financial statements won't tell you whether that company increased productivity, slid backwards, or just stood still. If productivity improvement is such a key factor in achieving economic improvement at a national, company or individual level, then a short detour to discuss this subject is in order.

The business environment includes both the physical and the financial. The physical side of the equation focuses on the relationship of the units of input—such as the time it takes to create a widget—to the units of output, which is the number of widgets. We can apply this basic idea to any process from making a computer to invoicing a customer. The physical equation deals only with the quantity of the input and the quantity of the output. It is the relationship between these physical factors that defines productivity. If you can get more output (widgets or invoices) with the same or less input (time) then we have a labor productivity gain. When we talk about the relationship between the price of the input—how much time costs—and the prices of the output, we are actually discussing price recovery. So, if workers' salaries are increased by four percent but the company cannot increase selling prices by at least that much, it has suffered a price recovery loss.

Once you multiply the quantities and prices of the inputs and outputs you are now dealing with dollars, and the relationship of the dollars of output to the dollars of input is profitability. In other words, sales dollars minus cost equals profitability. Figure 3.2 is a visual representation of these relationships. By understanding them, we can measure the two separate distinct influences on profitability. Then we can direct our efforts toward the areas that represent the greatest drain on profitability. In the lean world, we refer to these as opportunities.

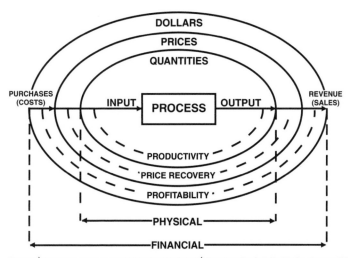

Source: ÒHow to Measure Productivity at the Firm Level,Ó American Productivity Center, January 1981

Figure 3.2 The Relationship of the Output to the Input (In Dollars) and Profitability

Focusing on each element of the cost of doing business will lead a team to look more clearly at each of the resources consumed.

Thus, the discussion surrounding the productivity of materials used can lead us to consider eliminating the causes of scrap and redesigning products to use less material. Thinking about prices paid for raw materials leads one to look at consolidating vendors in order to negotiate more competitive pricing and redesigning products to substitute less expensive materials. Likewise, the productivity of labor or any overhead element can be analyzed separately from both the quantity and the price portion of the equation.

The one thing that stands out clearly when these discussions take place is that in order to have productivity increase, there must be physical change. The change cannot be made solely in the numbers from accounting. Productivity cannot be improved through financial engineering. When we focus on physical change, we discover that the principal thrust is to eliminate waste. Thus, when we talk about kaizen or continuous improvement, we are talking about the relentless, never-ending pursuit of eliminating waste in all of its forms. Figure 3.3 is a list of the "Seven Sins of Waste" as identified in the Toyota Production System. Each of these wastes are created within some business processes and therefore can be identified, measured, and eliminated in order to increase productivity.

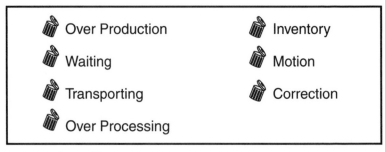

Figure 3.3 Seven Sins of Waste

Waste elimination generally requires a new mindset. Most people don't get up in the morning and say, "I think I'll go to work and create waste today." Dr. Edwards Deming, father of the modern quality movement, referred to most people as "willing workers" who were subjected to working in processes that had waste built in. Without calling it waste, most workers accept their wasteful practices as a normal routine. Eliminating waste requires an organization-wide mindset that:

1. Admits all processes contain waste
2. Puts tools in place to identify it in a non-blaming environment
3. Allows employees to eliminate it

Identifying waste

Identifying waste activities begins with separating all activities between those that add value and those that don't. This is easy to say but, in many cases, hard to do. How do we measure value? And valuable to whom? If a company is truly going to be transformed from an internal to an external (or customer) focus, then the core question is: Is it of value to the customer? If the customer would be willing to pay for it, it has value. If not, then it has no value. Unfortunately, some activities that don't have value by this definition must still be accomplished. A classic example of this is preparing tax returns. It adds no value to the product, but every business must do it. Once we have classified activities, what do we do with them? If the activity is adding value, or is required, we remove waste within the process by performing a kaizen. If there is no value or requirement, eliminate the activity.

▶

The barrier to the first mindset is something akin to pride of authorship. We ask, "How could I, a good and talented engineer, have created something bad?" The barrier embracing the second mindset is a culture of killing the messenger, and the barrier to the third is resistance to change.

Now that we have a good understanding of productivity and waste, we need to identify the performance measurements that will motivate the right behavior in order to achieve the desired results. Because each enterprise has some uniqueness, specific performance measures will differ between companies. Therefore, it is useful to identify the attributes of a good performance measurement system that can be applied to any organization. (Following this list, see our explanations for each rule.) All performance measures you select should:

Type of activity	Action
Value added	Kaizen
Non-value added, but required	Kaizen
Non-value added, not required	Eliminate

A common trap in separating non-value activities is to classify most of them as *required*. Before a non-value added activity is classified as required, the question "Required by whom?" must be asked. If the answer is internal to the enterprise, there is a good chance that it is not a requirement but a policy, and policy can be changed.

Even if the answer to that question is external to the enterprise (e.g., a customer requirement) it should not be blindly accepted. It still might only be a policy of the external organization and not a real requirement. For example, some of

▶

❑ Support the company's strategy

❑ Be relatively few in number

❑ Be mostly non-financial

❑ Be structured to motivate the right behavior

❑ Be simple and easy to understand

❑ Measure the process, not the people

❑ Measure actual results versus goals

❑ Not combine measures of different things into a single index

❑ Be timely, e.g., weekly, daily or hourly

❑ Show trend lines

❑ Be visual

Lantech's distributors always ordered machines in groups of five. When pressed, the distributors explained that, in the past, Lantech was not producing quickly enough for the end customer. As Lantech dramatically reduced lead time, the distributor was able to eliminate the batch ordering system—and as an added bonus, give customers the specific options they really wanted. The distributor could reduce their inventory of equipment and options. Admittedly, it is harder to get an external organization to change policy, but not impossible, especially if that organization is the customer and it can be demonstrated that the customer's non-value added policy is adding to the product cost. Most of the time, however, organizations find that non-value-added activities are strictly internal to the company and can be changed. In order to eliminate waste, physical change must occur; there is no way around this. As manufacturers become lean, some of the common physical changes include:

▶

Support the company's strategy: This is particularly important as the company transitions to lean business practices. Traditional metrics were created to support the traditional batch and queue business. Because many of the business practices must change dramatically in order to be lean, many of the traditional metrics will be misleading. If reduced lead time is key, make sure a metric about lead time is easy to collect and is reported frequently.

Be relatively few in number: Depending on the size of the organization, measurements need to be developed at various levels. At the lowest level are measurements that any employee can directly relate to. At the highest level are measurements that give information about the total enterprise. The number of intermediate levels will depend on the size of the organization. However, at each level the number of measurements should be few in number and focused on the activities that will yield the greatest results. The key is to focus on the process and produce reports that offer the most relevant information to the reader.

Be mostly non-financial: Since everyone in the organization needs to be involved in eliminating waste, and doing so requires physical change, most metrics should measure physical change. These metrics measure quantities, not dollars.

> ❑ Production grouped by product family
> ❑ Process layouts radically altered to facilitate flow production
> ❑ Internal stockrooms eliminated
> ❑ Material stored at the work cell in order to reduce movement
> ❑ Set-up time slashed

Be structured to motivate the right behavior: There are three ways to get better figures. First, you can improve the system. Second, you can distort the system and get the demanded results at the expense of other results. Third, you can distort the figures. In an organization where employees feel powerless to change the system, it is human nature for people to do whatever is necessary to make a metric appear to be improving, even if they do something that hurts the organization's performance in another area. A good example was an attempt to measure the productivity of pickers in a company's shipping department. The metric was in boxes picked per hour, for each picker. Many of the company's products are in boxes that are very small, but some are quite large. There was no control placed over how orders were picked, so each picker went through the orders and selected the ones with lots of small boxes. Naturally, the customer orders that had large product kept floating to the bottom of the pile. The productivity measure went up, but to the detriment of some customers. In the process of developing meaningful metrics, careful thought must be given to see if they could cause dysfunctional behavior. In other words, avoid the law of unintended consequences.

Be simple and easy to understand: If we expect employees to participate in waste elimination, the measures we establish must be meaningful to them. People must be able to relate an improvement in their work to an improvement in the metric. That means each and every person who is part of the process should know how to be part of the solution. If an employee does something to make the process better, it should show up in the measure.

Measure the process, not the people: Recognizing Dr. Demings' depiction of the "willing worker" and the belief that bad processes—not bad people—create waste, the measurements must focus on the process. Once we try to measure people, we are sending a message that we are trying to affix blame and will send people running for cover and making excuses. By focusing on the process, employees can readily participate in identifying waste in a non-threatening way.

Set ambitious goals and measure actual results: To say simply that we want to improve does not give people an understanding of how far they need to go. Setting a goal for modest improvements allow people to achieve those levels by doing what they currently do a bit better. In order to get people to understand that they must dramatically change they way they work, management needs to establish stretch goals and measure actual results against those goals.

Do not combine measures of different things into a single index: It is easier for people to understand what they have to do if the measure is not bundled into a complex equation and each element that goes into a ratio is measured separately and has separate goals. If the metric has too many elements going into it, it loses its meaning and employees no longer understand what must be done to improve.

Be timely, e.g. weekly, daily or hourly: One of the primary uses of performance measurements is to trigger management to take corrective action when it becomes apparent that a goal is not going to be met. For example, it does not help customer service if we know tomorrow that we didn't make today's production schedule. By measuring production against a plan based on takt time, and identifying reasons throughout the day for any shortfall—hourly or more frequently—management can take corrective action before the day is finished.

Show trend lines: One of the underlying themes of continuous improvement is that it is, of course, never ending. We want to perform better today than we did yesterday. Thus, every performance measurement chart should show not only the actual results and goal for this period, but also the trend over a longer period of time to demonstrate continuous improvement.

Be visual: If it is worth measuring, it should be displayed in a way that everyone can see. When management walks into any work area, it should be readily apparent what is important for that area by what they measure. Management should also see, at a glance, where the area stands against its goals, any improvement over time and reasons for a shortfall in performance—all without asking questions. The most commonly used analogy is that of a sporting event, where everyone's eyes return again and again to the scoreboard. Visual displays of the performance measures are our scoreboards.

Performance Measures: Categories and Explanations

Earlier we discussed the need to develop metrics that would have a positive impact on ROI, which employees could relate to within their specific jobs. Since we have now defined the attributes of a good performance measurement system and recognize that different businesses may identify different things to measure, we can offer a kind of deli menu of performance measurements. Just remember as you read the following chart that every business should only choose to measure that which is critical to the strategic objectives. Measure too many things at once and the system becomes swamped.

51

REAL NUMBERS

Customer Satisfaction & Responsiveness	2000	2001	2002 Goal	2002 Final
Customer Satisfaction Index				
Customer Return Percentage				
Delivery Performance				
Average Quoted Lead Time				
Late Shipments:				
Measured in $				
Measured by # Parts Affected				
Measured by # Customers Affected				
Abandoned Customer Phone Calls %				
Custom Quotes Completed Within 24 Hours %				

Flexibility & Responsiveness	2000	2001	2002 Goal	2002 Final
Defects Per 1,000 Units				
Performance to Takt Time				
Percentage of Time Each Cell Meets Takt Time				
Average First-Pass Yield Percentage				
Raw Material Inventory $				
WIP Inventory $				
Finished Goods Inventory $				
Total Inventory, Days on Hand				

Cost & Productivity	2000	2001	2002 Goal	2002 Final
Rate of Productivity Growth				
Constant $ Sales Per Employee				
Absenteeism				
Unplanned Downtime				

Safety & Ergonomics	2000	2001	2002 Goal	2002 Final
Injuries				
Medical Costs Per 100 Associates				
Lost-time Accidents				

Financial Performance	2000	2001	2002 Goal	2002 Final
Net Sales				
Operating Income as Percent of Sales				
R&D Cost as Percent of Sales				
Percent of Sales from New Products				
Capital Investment as Percent of Sales				
■ % For New Products				
■ % For Capacity				
■ % For Safety, Environmental, etc.				
Working Capital as Percent of Sales				

Customer Satisfaction & Responsiveness

Customer Satisfaction Index: Each company's index will be different, based on what value they uniquely bring to the customer. For a computer maker like Gateway or Dell, for instance, important values would be delivery times, ease of ordering and repair turnaround. A major hotel chain would look closely at how many guests return each year.

Customer Return Rate: This tells manufacturing how products fare in the field, indicating the health of the process.

Delivery Performance: This is an external measurement, showing on-time delivery rates.

53

Average Quoted Lead Time: Becoming lean means slashing lead time. Keeping track of this number reveals whether all aspects of the business are taking new capabilities directly to the customer.

Late Shipments, Measured in Dollars, # Parts Affected, # of Customers Affected: Wiremold uses all three measures. The number of parts affected and number of customers affected reveals total impact in the market. Measurement in dollars shows management precisely why revenue was not achieved this month.

Abandoned Customer Phone Calls: Program your phone system to measure how many callers hang up before reaching a representative. When the abandon rate crosses an acceptable threshold, your customers are probably frustrated. Consider tracking the questions asked, looking for similar questions that might be answered up front. Also reassess which calls get priority.

❑ Call Backs. What percentage of questions does not require a call back from a client services representative? This is a good indicator of whether your representatives have the most useful information at hand.

Custom Quotes Completed Within 24 Hours: Most companies take days or a week to tell their valued customer how much a custom solution costs. Become dedicated to giving true customer service and providing it within 24 hours.

Flexibility & Responsiveness

Defects Per 1,000 Units: For high-ticket items, such as capital goods, you might track this by Defects Per 100 Units. This is most effectively tracked when producers have good after-sales contact with customers.

Performance to Takt: This is an internal measurement, reflecting how well the organization performs to takt time.

Percentage of Time Each Working Cell Meets Takt Time: Tracking on an hourly basis how effectively each cell is meeting the customer requirements (i.e., within takt time), will help pinpoint problem areas more precisely.

Average First Pass Yield: This highlights process problems and allows managers to focus improvements.

Raw Material Inventory: Are you ordering too much of one thing from your suppliers? Are you paying extra warehousing fees when you could receive smaller, more frequent shipments? Keep an eye on this data to find out.

WIP (Work In Process) Inventory: Search for your process bottlenecks in the amount of work that piles up between processes.

Finished Goods Inventory: Are you really producing to customer demand? Is your forecasting wrong or your shipping process broken? This metric will alert you to questions that need to be asked.

Total Inventory, Days On Hand: As this dollar figure shrinks, you are liberating cash to be used in other, more important areas: innovation, new products, acquisition or grabbing new market share.

Product Development Lead Time: Anyone making products for consumers knows how critical this measure is, showing how quickly you can get new ideas to market.

Cost & Productivity

Rate of Productivity Growth: A lean company shoots for 8-15 percent productivity growth per year.

Constant $ Sales Per Employee: Strip away the fluctuations of price and keep a constant measure. This is a common view of real productivity.

Absenteeism: This is not just a financial measure, but also an emotional one—telling you if your employees are engaged and taking personal responsibility. If you want the trend line to go upwards with good news, call it *presenteeism.*

Unplanned Downtime: Keeping good data at the cell level— with hour-by-hour charts, for instance—maintains a steady vigilance on this important metric.

Safety & Ergonomics

Injuries: Accidents are also defects. Work accidents create waste such as lost time and medical bills, not to mention physical suffering for the employee. As with a defect, when an accident occurs we must perform a root-cause analysis to determine the real cause and avoid it in the future.

Medical Costs Per 100 Associates

Lost-time Accidents: This should separate the serious accidents from the everyday hurts.

Financial Performance

Net Sales

Operating Cost as Percent of Sales: An efficiency measure, to be tracked on a continuum.

Research and Development as Percent of Sales: Are you investing in the future?

Percent of Sales From New Products: Keep an eye on whether R&D efforts are paying off.

Capital Investment as Percent of Sales: This number alone would not tell an organization enough about trends. But break down capital investments for new products, capacity and safety or environmental costs, and you've got real information. As a company goes lean, there should be a dramatic shift over time toward capital investment in new products. In the early years, investment in capacity should drop impressively while kaizen activities free up unused capacity.

Working Capital as a Percent of Sales: As cash is more effectively utilized, this percentage will decrease. This percentage can also be used as a macro number for cash planning. For example, if sales are expected to grow by $1 million and the working capital percentage is 20 percent, then expect to raise $200,000 in cash to support working capital.

TIP : STRUCTURE YOUR METRICS SO THAT THE POSITIVE TRENDS RESULT IN AN UPWARD LINE.

The goal of performance measurement should be to manage processes, not results. In organizations that manage results, we find behaviors that accommodate the symptoms of problems by adding more non-value added activities, distorting the system and achieving results at the expense of other areas. In most cases, managing results creates self-deception. In the worst cases, organizations go as far as creating false financial statements.

Once an organization changes its orientation from managing results to managing processes—and is supported by an intelligent performance measurement system—employees will feel free to publicly identify defects and waste without fear. This is not about simply generating reports. This is about establishing a robust mechanism for instituting process improvement and creating an environment in which true long term improvements can be achieved.

4

STREAMLINING THE PROCESS

I shall enjoy my freedom from the tyranny of the In and Out boxes.

S. Dillon Ripley, on his retirement after 20 years
as secretary of the Smithsonian Institution.

IN ORDER TO ACHIEVE THE POSITION of valued business partner,
we first must gain our freedom from drudgery. So let's move on
to the action-oriented activities that will get us there. The ideas
we offer here for eliminating the waste of time and energy that
goes into transactions chasing have worked well in businesses of
different sizes. Whether they will work in yours depends partly
on business strategies, partly on commitment. At the end, we
hope to turn those triangles from Chapter Two upside down.

In any career, taking action and making change can be the
most fun and fulfilling part of the work. When it's fun, it's also

contagious. Like a chain reaction, change and continuous improvement catch on and become not only accepted in the workplace, but expected.

Change can take place in many forums. Each of the following forum types share vital ingredients: a designated place and time where an open exchange of ideas is encouraged, where there is a sense of importance to the work and a knowledge that whatever comes out of the forum will be taken seriously.

❑ Major projects. Usually spread over a significant time, major projects generally require that information be collected from many sources. A substantial time investment usually occurs up front while parameters are identified and agreed upon, but after the kick-off, the commitment is part-time only.

❑ A kaizen breakthrough event is familiar to the lean organization. This forum brings together eight to 15 individuals from different departments for three to five days to work full-time on improving a process. After training in lean principles, the team observes, collects data and brainstorms before implementing and testing improvements, all during the same week. Post-kaizen refinements and 30-day homework assignments ensure that improvements are fixed into the process.

❑ The Hot Spot, or point kaizen, is usually a one- or two-day event utilizing the full time and problem-solving attention of six to 10 people. This can be one small snarl of an issue or one that needs a team's muscle to implement. One recent Hot Spot at Lantech addressed the question: When a machine's design is changed, how are people notified of product improvements? The team discovered that design-change notices were indeed circulated—but so frequently that notices were perceived as an annoyance, rather than informative. Instead of distributing 500 engineering change notices per month, the team identified a more manageable 60 average monthly notices that were relevant.

❑ Individual daily improvements are the most common variety, practiced continually in a lean environment.

Modern companies are most familiar with the first and last forums: large projects and individual improvements. Learning to use kaizen events and Hot Spots are very useful for businesses looking for a way to supercharge the change environment. When a large commitment of time and resources are dedicated to improvement activities, it sends a strong message that change is not only acceptable, but expected. Kaizen events and Hot Spots are also physically visible to the workforce. Hard-working teams are not just a few people in a meeting room for an hour every week, but a busy cluster of people usually working for several days in a visible location, implementing change.

Executive commitment and the visibility of improvement work will be of central importance to any company that wishes to send a clear message for change. At Wiremold, there is an annual President's Kaizen whereby the executives from all of its companies gather at one site to participate in a three- or four-day kaizen event. This sends a clear message: "Do as I do, not just as I say." No matter how clear the message, however, do not expect that message to be identically received by all associates. Mostly, we find that the change message is received in one of three ways.

Some people come naturally to change, especially when the road ahead looks clear and safe. Those people will embrace the new way and become what we call *early adopters* or, as we affectionately call them, *zealots*. No team is ever populated exclusively with change zealots. If we support the early adopters we have, however, they can be a lot of fun and help pull the footdraggers into the change environment.

The majority of us fall into a middle category. We carefully watch our surroundings to ascertain what is safe and acceptable behavior. Think about entering a new acquaintance's home or a new church or restaurant. At times like this, our social radar is usually turned up high to pick up clues about any new rules or expectations, and then we play along with the behavioral norm. But on the inside, we might spend a good deal of time deciding if we want to truly embrace the new friend or church or work environment. The new way is inevitably weighed against personal values and self-interest. So if we want to be successful at work, for instance, and all the cues tell us that improvement and change are applauded, we are far more likely to eventually embrace change and improvement and use whatever innate talents we have to advance the cause.

Other people are hierarchical. For these people, the boss needs to have complete control. Hierarchies are instantly recognizable due to the bottleneck on top, because all communication and decisions must be filtered through the boss. In the hierarchical world view, bosses are assumed smarter than all other team members by default. Naturally, the distinction of being the boss is clung to dearly. We have found that most often, these people are threatened by change and will find a thousand ways to undermine transformation. It takes strength and commitment to overcome the efforts of people who don't want to change. Be aware of the bad influence these people can have on the team. Because these concrete heads[5] can undermine the confidence of team members and usually have a very loud voice based on traditional attitudes in the company, be sure they are not making rules or setting the tone. A boss can drive some improvements, of course. In a hierarchy, the boss will plan the change and order the implementation and create an environment where associates wait to be told what to do instead of employing their own brains and creativity to create innovation.

What we advocate is an environment where leaders contribute ideas and suggestions on nearly equal footing with the team. A leader's hands are not tied, but we must also respect the atmosphere of open communication being created. In short, be careful not to squash anyone.

One excellent way of getting everyone involved in daily improvements, right from the beginning, is to institute a program like Q52. Jean first implemented this quality improvement initiative at a large computer maker in the 1980s in which process improvements—measurable and written down—are delivered every week of the year. What Jean asked from each of her team members was a personal commitment to look for ideas both small and large that could be implemented to reduce cost, increase quality, decrease process steps, reduce time, or increase customer satisfaction.

The guidelines were purposefully simple. When a team member improved something, that person wrote it down in a couple of

---

5 A term used within the lean world for change-resistant colleagues.

sentences or paragraphs that described what was changed and the impact it had. Those sentences and pages were then turned over to one person who kept a count and offered quick monthly reports. The person who had the idea and implemented it was the one to report it, but the names of other people involved could also be reported.

The only real criterion was that the improvement had to be implemented. Having a good idea is not enough because, simply put, the benefit is not derived until the deed is done. On the other hand, there was no differentiation between big ideas and smaller ideas with lesser impact. It is important to count improvements, big and small, all the same to emphasize the more important concept: do it every day. It might be difficult sometimes to keep that sense of balance, but remember that if more credit is given for big ideas, people will develop a tendency to overlook the small items and wait for the big one. In this atmosphere of waiting for *the big one,* the true value of programs like Q52—taking lots of small steps forward—is lost. One good idea, implemented and set in place by the worker affected, is compounded by every good idea that comes after.

In the colonial city of Queretaro, Mexico, where Black & Decker Household Products are manufactured, urging employees to come forward with improvement ideas has become a mainstay of the operation and is called *Teian.* Like Q52, the parameters are simple: improvement ideas, generated by the plant's 2,400 employees are collected, counted, implemented when appropriate, and rewarded. In this large operation, tracking Teian is also done on a grand scale.

Driving into the employee parking lot, a huge, colorful sign reminds workers of how many good ideas were generated this month, as compared to last month. Teian metrics are included in every operations manager's report; every area is expected to produce a minimum number of employee improvements per year. The message is firm and constant: employee involvement and ideas are crucial.

Managers at Black & Decker Household Products, which is now owned by Applica, Inc., credit their ongoing lean initiative, kaizen breakthroughs and Teian with some great metrics. In 1995, the plant had a scrap rate of 4 percent; now it is 0.4 percent. Absenteeism was 5 to 6 percent; today it hovers at 2 to 3 percent. Output has doubled with just 20 percent more employees and they have the largest small appliances market share in every country in which they sell.

For everyday improvements to work, it is important to avoid judgments on worthiness. When there is one judge to decide if an idea is good enough, some team members will avoid making or documenting improvements—no matter how obvious or straightforward—for fear of group ridicule. Q52 and Teian programs emphasize that every step forward is worthy of credit and adds to the overall effectiveness of the team.

Still, we are left with the question of how to acknowledge and celebrate the great ideas being implemented. At the Black & Decker plant, managers offer small prizes for implemented ideas, from pens to shirts and hats with company logos, but they focus on discipline. At Lantech, Jean has had some successes and some failures with encouragement and enabling participation.

Jean's team decided early on not to count the improvements made by each person individually because they believed it could lead to dangerous territory. (Do great ideas count for double? Are small improvements only worth half?) At one time, Lantech gave each person a letter of the word QUALITY for every improvement or customer-satisfying event. Once the word quality was spelled out, the associate got a small certificate for lunch. Guess what happened? At first it worked fine. Then one or two people who were good at spotting improvement opportunities and getting things done started getting lots of letters and earning lunches. A little competition started up between the top producers, which unintentionally left others out. Those people not competing polarized themselves and, instead of jumping in, they quit participating all together. Rushing to the opposite position, this faction asserted that any improvements were "just doing my job." This was sometimes a false modesty; but more important, it was a passive way of putting down those who were competing. Before long, the value of a letter was low and the program fell from favor. Personal competition, it was clear, was not working.

Having fun as a group did work, however. On the heels of those QUALITY lunches, Jean started an office pool. At the beginning of each year, everyone guesses how many Q52s they will get as a team that year and writes the number down on a slip of paper. All the slips go into an envelope that is sealed and stuck on a bulletin board for the year. On the anniversary, after all the Q52s are turned in and tallied, the envelope is opened. No one ever remembers what he or she guessed, but everyone cheers the person who came closest and the winner gets a goofy trophy. For a couple of years, the prize was one of Jean's old athletic trophies with a piece of duct tape over the name and year. But Jean claims she wasn't that great of an athlete, and she soon ran out of trophies. She started handing out oddball home crafts instead. One person got a stuffed fish on a piece of wood; another, an antique plate with the occasion spelled out in magic marker. The stranger the trophy, the more treasured they became. And it's all for a lucky guess.

Wiremold has a suggestion system that gives associates one point for making a suggestion and another point when it is implemented. Points are given for just making a suggestion in order to encourage new thinking. Like Lantech, no differentiation is made between small and large suggestions. Associates can collect their points and then cash them in for gifts from a gift catalogue, much like the old Green Stamp programs. The more points accumulated, the larger the gift received. In addition, each quarter a raffle is held and each associate has one ticket in the raffle for each suggestion made during the quarter. Wiremold, like Applica's plant in Queretaro, also tracks the number of suggestions made by individual and by team in order to encourage 100 percent participation.

The point is, with any properly designed suggestion system, everyone becomes a change agent. Once we acknowledge that each and every associate knows his or her own work process well enough to substantially improve the process, we begin to become a team instead of a hierarchy. When individuals know they can create change, power is rebalanced very quickly. When the message is sent that change is not just encouraged, it is expected, it becomes clear that those who do not improve will not be successful.

Before we get to specific examples of Q52-type projects, two general types of improvement should be discussed: paper and integration.

Paper is a barrier. Think about that piece of paper with vital information that was just distributed to 10 people. Every person can see the information, but then something changes that five of the original 10 people need to know right away, plus seven others should be informed. That piece of paper can only be in one place at a time, even though many might need the information it has, and its information is unchangeable. Get that information online—or at the very least onto large, easy-to-read posters, publicly displayed—and everyone has access to information.

We're not talking about a paperless office; we are moving toward a less-paper office. Pick the pieces of information that are most important and reconsider the distribution methods. If the data is made available to all, there is no sense in sitting down to figure out who needs that data and when. When information is generally available within an organization, people can pull the data when needed, instead of passively having it pushed upon them. In the end there is less filing, less paper shuffling.

Ensuring that information is available to whoever needs it and is presented logically leads us to a less-paper office—and it leads to systems integration.

At any one time, the average manufacturing business probably has at least four distinct and discrete systems: manufacturing, sales, accounting and engineering. In the average week, each department spends untold hours entering information into their own system, for their own understanding and use. Then, in effect, the department hoards it. Integration means spending the money, acquiring the expertise and thinking deeply about the system of information flow so that we can logically move information from one module to another without human intervention.

Nobody should re-enter data. Sales should be able to reach through the system and pull shipping and manufacturing information, just as manufacturing needs to pull the customer service or accounting data they require to make intelligent decisions.

With an integrated system, the processes that live downstream can proactively look up to see what's coming at them. For example, international shipments usually require additional paperwork for shipping and invoicing. By creating an alert in the system, we can see when a shipment of that type is coming—next week, day or hour—and get the extra work performed early, avoiding delays. The key is identical information, available to everyone.

Let's move on to some examples of changes we made in each of our business functions. A traditional accounting textbook would organize these ideas by accounting functions: accounts payable, equity, accounts receivable and taxes. Instead, we organized these ideas based on the business process they illustrate or support because one of the key premises of this book is that accounting work is not a goal separate from the business.

All businesses, whether manufacturing or service-oriented, consist of these processes and all are ripe for improvement. The people with accounting expertise are there to support the business through analysis and consulting, as well as transactional processing. Recognition of the accounting transaction as a part of the business process is important because it can help eliminate barriers to waste, not only in accounting but also in the business process itself. The business process has been changing in many companies and sometimes improvement has been blocked due to barriers created by accounting. This is the last thing we want. So let's look at the work from a business process perspective and see what overall waste elimination and improvement opportunities exist.

Waste exists in every process. Think about the entire work process: producing the work, waiting to work, moving work, correcting work and reworking the work. All activities other than doing the work are candidates for change or elimination.

To help you think about changes that can be made, we offer the following examples of changes we have made in hopes of spurring you to action. Some might appear difficult and others remarkably simple—even simple-minded. But even the most elementary improvements can be both difficult and immensely valuable in an organization.

Just remember, this is a game of singles, not home runs.

Order, Ship, Bill & Collect:

Activities relating to accepting orders, filling the orders, invoicing the customer and collecting the money for the order.

Order entry: In moving from a *push* to a *pull* scheduling environment, the factory must have clear visibility to customer orders on a timely basis. Most systems are not designed for this since the factory produces to a schedule based on a forecast.

The first kaizen done at Wiremold in 1991 was on the order entry system. This was necessary to do before any changes were made in the factory. In addition, new-order information is usually not part of the financial documents. However, the flow of new orders is the most critical information you can gather about future financial performance. Add it to your financial statements right above shipments or revenue. Or go a step further and have the integrated system post that information directly to the general ledger as orders are entered. Later, change orders can be added and the results of your reporting can be seen every day.

Cash collection information: If you are a small company, sometimes it is too expensive to get same-day, online cash receipt information from the bank. But managers may want same-day information on the last day of the month to close the books quickly. Tailor your agreement with the bank to courier the information to you on that day only. On the other days, let the mail deliver receipts.

International Invoices: International customers frequently need to receive an original invoice, but regular mail service takes too long or can be unreliable in some countries. Lantech converted the invoices to a format that could not be edited at the customer site, using Adobe Acrobat software, and now all invoices are emailed for the customer to print at their discretion.

Sales Tax Procedures: One of the most error-prone and time-consuming processes, with no value added for the customer, is calculating and charging sales tax. To minimize time and errors, ensure that sales tax information is correct when the order is initially taken. At Lantech, the sales-tax clerk looks at the orders entered each day to make sure they are correct. If she is unsure of the rate required for a specific address, she looks up the address using a handy Internet site that finds for her the exact tax jurisdiction. This eliminates changes later, ensuring that it is invoiced correctly and assists the customer in paying quickly. If a customer does not pay the sales tax, have the clerk posting cash receipts immediately contact the customer to request a sales-tax exemption certificate or request final payment. The key is to do a transaction once and be done.

Mailing Invoices: To reduce the time spent folding, stuffing and mailing invoices, create a Pareto chart of all outgoing invoice addresses. Focus on the largest volume customers first and find ways to reduce the amount of paperwork sent. Perhaps invoices can be faxed daily or weekly, and the original thrown out to avoid duplicates at the customer site. This gets the invoice in the hands of the customer faster, which hopefully will mean faster payment. In addition, don't print an internal file copy, but rely on the electronic database.

Collection Calls: Reforming cash collections is tough, because the customer is the one who controls what bills are paid. But we can control how often we contact that customer. For instance, a company that needs to increase the number of collection calls made on a daily basis needs to keep the goal in front of the clerks. Use a visual cue, like two glass jars with large marbles; one jar depicts the number of calls the clerk needs to make, the other shows calls made. Each time she makes a call, she moves a marble to the other jar. The clerk can then self-monitor and see the progress being made each day.

Sales Records: Electronically attach or clip documents to the order so everyone using the order can see all documents. These might include the commercial invoice, bill of lading, purchase order or single sales tax exemption certificates.

Collection Information: Look at how reports are used and sort data in that order. For instance, the list of customer balances is used in alphabetical order by name, instead of by customer number. So, change your report. A quick review of how reports—online or paper copies—are used can yield some good improvements.

Purchase, Receive and Pay:

Activities related to purchasing inventory and non-inventory items, receiving purchased goods and paying suppliers.

Pay Suppliers Electronically: To reduce the hassle of printing and mailing checks, receiving canceled checks and dealing with lost checks, ask your suppliers for the bank information where payments can be sent. This also allows you to more precisely control when funds transfer.

Invoice Processing: One of the most time-consuming accounting processes is paying invoices. We receive invoices, match them to the purchase order, make sure the items were received and get approval to pay the invoice from someone with authority. This process is full of improvement opportunities. One dramatic improvement is to stop collecting invoices for materials received frequently from a supplier-partner. In a lean environment, operations will begin ordering in smaller and smaller batches (often using a nearly automatic method of ordering called kanban), dramatically increasing the number of invoices received. Instead of paying for every invoiced delivery, pay the vendor for materials at the agreed upon purchase-order price when materials are received, eliminating the invoice. Purchasing will have to get involved and it is usually best to implement one supplier at a time.

Early Pay Discounts: Look at the interest rate you are passing up when you do not take early-pay discounts and decide how much of a discount you need to receive in order to make the early payment. A common mistake is applying the early pay to the total amount of the check. Instead, only apply the discount to new items and don't apply it to the credits you might have with the supplier.

Bench Stock and Office Supplies: For high-volume, very low-cost items (like nuts and bolts on your product or pens and paper in the office) consider working with one supplier who will restock your parts bins on a daily basis. Then have the supplier bill you on a monthly basis only for the items stocked. This is a good example of where the risk of overpaying for the item is low, and the processing cost of procuring the item is much too high. It is unlikely that a supplier with a large percentage of your parts business will over bill the company and the cost of avoiding that risk—counted in purchase orders, approvals, matching receipts and multiple invoices for nuts and bolts—can be very high.

Payment Checks: Eliminate special typing on checks being sent out by using a miscellaneous field in your software system that can automatically print on your check remittance.

Invoice Processing: Typically, a receptionist or mailroom clerk sorts the mail every day and might automatically send all invoices to accounting. Accounting sorts through the invoices again, looking for what can be paid and what needs outside approval. If the clerk or receptionist can sort the invoices that need approval first and send them to the proper person, one handling process is eliminated.

Cancelled Checks: Use tools available at the bank, such as canceled checks on CD-ROMs to cut down on physical documents and shuffling through them. With records on CDs, accountants can search for documents electronically and keep a years' worth of records in the same space as a week's worth of cancelled checks.

Research: The prime benefit of an integrated system is being able to drill down on a specific item to confirm accuracy of accounts. For example, you should be able to open an electronic version of a customer's bill and click on certain fields to see all the background information. An order number, for instance, could reveal who placed the order and delivery date requested. Going to the part-number field should reveal if the part is available. When considering whether to issue a credit, this is all valuable information.

Hire, Pay and Benefits

All activities related to hiring employees, paying their salaries and personal expenses, and procuring and processing benefits.

Payroll General Ledger Entry: Eliminate manual re-entry of payroll results to the general ledger, if you outsource payroll. Instead, import a file from your payroll service. This will help you close the books more quickly and have the information easily accessible throughout the month.

Expense Reports: Create an online expense report. Or put a common spreadsheet in an electronic file that is accessible to all and includes the account number for ease of entering.

Pay Changes: Calculate the pay increase using a spreadsheet and then upload the spreadsheet file to your payroll processing service to eliminate keying individual increase amounts manually.

Compensation Administration: Lantech uses a matrix of pay increases based on range penetration and performance. Pay changes are calculated based on a person's performance rating and on where their current pay is compared to the pay range. The application of those increases are now performed in accounting instead of being figured—and possibly fumbled— by every team leader. This results in less time spent overall and fewer errors in calculation.

Benefits Costs: Instead of breaking down your benefit bills and payroll taxes (medical insurance premiums, dental bills, self insurance bills, Social Security taxes, local taxes, etc.) by cost center or department, create one cost center for all benefits costs. Considering the fact that individual cost centers cannot directly effect the cost of benefits, try not to allocate benefits to cost centers. If you feel that you must allocate, do so as a percentage of pay. This eliminates hours spent splitting up cost precisely, when only accurate information is needed. The benefits cost center can be used to evaluate and manage the total benefits cost.

Contract Management: Third-party vendors provide many benefits. Check that vendors are complying with their contracts. If the dental program has a maximum benefit, look at the reports to make sure that the insurance company is not paying more than the maximum. If your workers' compensation plan gives a discount for a drug-free workplace policy, make sure they know if you have one. These sound so simple, but someone has to look at it to ensure the company receives the right benefit costs, and sometimes, pay dirt is waiting in contract compliance.

Taxes, Audits and Other Regulatory Requirements

Tax Filing: Doing the job in a timely manner reduces interest and penalty payments. Review the returns to make sure excess payments are returned rather than being applied to the next year. Your company, not the government, should be earning interest on that overpayment money.

Submitting Tax Returns: Most companies owe information to a lot of different tax authorities and the careful accountant sends it via certified mail to keep a clear record. But sending all those reports via certified mail is time-consuming and boring work. Initially, Lantech created a small file with all the addresses for every state, which made for easier printing. Now, it's possible to send most returns and fees through each state's electronic cash receipts process. It takes time to set up, but once done, it is secure and easy to track.

Taxes Liability: Create a recurring spreadsheet (or report within your integrated systems) to calculate estimates of the items that are treated differently for tax purposes than for GAAP. This can give you a quick report for estimating tax liability.

Audit Reports: Ensure that reports created for the auditors are in the same format that you use for account reconciliation throughout the year, and that auditors have agreed to work with this format. This avoids duplicate reports and it makes preparing for the audit very simple.

Reporting: For the company with a non-integrated system, spreadsheet software can be your best friend. Transfer data out of one system electronically into a spreadsheet, manipulate it there, and then transfer out to the non-integrated module. For instance, if you want your financials divided by product line and your sales system does not segregate product line sales, download all sales entries and use the spreadsheet software to resort it by product line. Subtotal your columns, then put the results of the reports into the general ledger.

To pull an accounting department together to work as a team, it is also important to take a good hard look at how we arrange ourselves. Most offices look like cube farms—with all the work areas set in faceless rows, concealing team members and their work from one another. Even the team leader generally cannot see if one person is frantic and strangled with work while another is surfing the Internet to kill time. Worse yet, cubicles kill the open communication that allows a two-second question—the questions that can be answered without really interrupting, but that help fill in the details of our work.

Instead, we recommend that offices be set up in such a way that team members can easily see and speak to one another. Some have had great success with lower cubicle walls. Others have turned the cube inside out, creating larger common areas for discrete teams (see Figure 4.1).

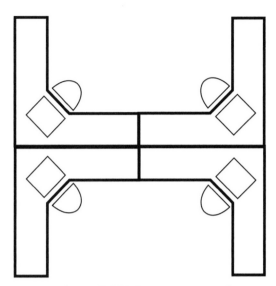

Figure 4.1 Lower Cubicle Walls and Shared Spaces Create Visual Control

With team members speaking to each other and seeing one another's work flow, they will also see opportunities to rebalance work loads and cross-train without too much prompting. Partly, this is a morale issue. Cubicles have become so expected that we don't even hear the complaints anymore. Work and tedium go hand in glove, right? Not necessarily. For companies particularly interested in retaining employees, having a little fun and socializing at work can become a critical issue. Accountants especially need to be able to look up and chat a little in order to relieve themselves of the streams of numbers that occupy their days. A little fun at work means a happier, more stable team, who might socialize a little at their desks—where they can still answer the phone and work—and won't be off to the break room at every opportunity.

If a department can rid itself of cubicles altogether, it is then free to relocate desks into more logical patterns, related to information flow rather than simple space requirements. Most companies have all the compliance people sitting together, and all the credit-check clerks in a clump. At Lantech, Jean rearranged desks to mimic the U-shaped cell favored by lean manufacturing. Looking at how work transferred from one person to another, she moved the invoice clerk next to the sales-tax clerk, both of them facing the person doing collections and added to the area a visual board showing sales and cash information (see Figure 4.2) Now, when the person doing collections has questions about an invoice, or the sales tax clerk has a question about a customer in California who owed a large amount of back sales tax, he only needs to raise his voice to normal speaking tones to get a question answered. A clerk specializing in medical insurance might sit next to a payroll clerk and those who deal with different aspects of computer leasing might have their own area.

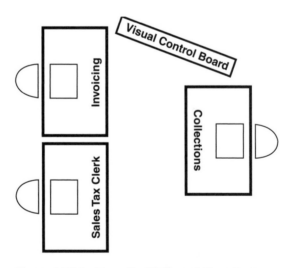

Figure 4.2 Take Down the Walls and Move Desks into Patterns that Reflect Work Flow

This configuration also encourages cross training, which should not stop at the edge of the factory floor.

"We think cross-training is vitally important," says CFO Greg Flint of the country's premiere granite processing company, Minnesota's Cold Spring Granite. "We're focusing on one-piece flow, no matter the activity. So, our belief is that all clerks should be able to perform all jobs.

"For instance, when the mail comes to accounting in most organizations, some pieces will go to the tax specialist or collections or accounts receivable. We want any clerk to be able to pick up the mail and deal with each piece—to pick it up and put it down once and be done with it. It's the same idea as in our plants; we want people to multi-task."

At Cold Spring Granite, a cross-training matrix is posted in the department so that anyone can tell, at a glance, how Flint is managing the process. Across the top of the matrix is the list of tasks that need to be performed in his department. Down the side are the employees. An "O" in one of the central squares means the person is in training. A partial fill-in means the clerk has been trained, but cannot yet perform to cycle-time. If the "O" is filled in by two-thirds, the clerk can do it to cycle time and a total fill-in means the clerk can train others on the task. The only other marks are a few crossed-out squares, which show the spots where cross-training will not occur because, as Flint points out, the need for internal controls means you must sometimes be selective. For instance, an accounts payable clerk should not also be in charge of creating vendor contracts.

The real benefit of cross training is flexibility. When the entire department can respond to fluctuations in demand during the month, you have eliminated the waste that occurs when some people are working too fast and others are killing time.

With waste eliminated from processes, here are some new, more value-added activities you can include:

❑ Look at warehouse rent charges and then visit the site to ensure all the square footage being paid for is used. At Lantech, the bill was reduced by 95 percent when it was analyzed how much space was going unused.

❑ Consider in-sourcing activities, such as payroll or lead generation.

❑ Assign your accountants to different product teams to help the teams understand the economic impact of the decisions they make.

In order to be more consultative we, as an entire team, must also understand more about the purpose of the business and how it is performing. One technique to accomplish this is a monthly team meeting to discuss the financial and performance metrics of the business and of the accounting team. It is a blend of business performance and accounting performance. Every person on the team presents information about their area, using trend reports for performance over time, comparison charts to show performance against a target or budget, a Pareto chart to show results in order of frequency, or some other comparative information. Discuss the results of the month and any key drivers of that result. Some examples of a recent month's agenda topics include:

1. Order entry, shipments and profit results
2. Cash balance
3. Number of invoices processed
4. Cash discounts taken
5. Number of days to close
6. List of post-close entries
7. Percentage of orders reviewed with incorrect sales tax information
8. Warranty performance
9. Cash receipts
10. DSO (Days Sales Outstanding) by sales channel
11. Inventory days supply on hand
12. Improvements made in past month
13. Employee receivables aging
14. Suppliers added in last month
15. Backlog by product line

Each person is encouraged to ask questions for understanding, or make suggestions for improvement. There is a lot of value in this meeting: a team member reflects on the content of her job while preparing the metrics and also gets exposed to others' work. Common problems can be identified and awareness is raised about the effects of everyone's work. These meetings also create a forum for discussing issues and offering suggestions for improvement that are focused on the work, not the person. This hour-long meeting can pay huge benefits in creating the under-pinnings of a change environment.

The point is to get started: in meetings and individually, even if the steps seem small. With small steps, with little improvements that we recognize, with efforts that we cheer, we begin to change our culture and our work lives. With team members empowered to make changes, with colleagues that take ownership of their processes in an atmosphere of positive change, we will be on the path to becoming valued business partners—no longer a slave to transactions.

5

COST MANAGEMENT VS. COST ACCOUNTING

COMPANIES THAT BEGIN THE TRANSITION from batch and queue to lean manufacturing always run into problems with accounting systems, with the biggest issue being cost accounting. As teams of employees tear out old processes, move equipment, cut waste and continue to do this over time, determining the cost of any one product becomes difficult. In fact, it becomes more frustrating with each improvement. The average accountant may end up feeling like Oscar Wilde's man who knows the cost of everything but the value of nothing. And he's right.

Instead of cost accounting, the lean accountant's focus should be on cost management, which includes a different kind of cost accounting. We have learned that it is far less important to know the cost of making an individual product than it is to manage the costs of the business as a whole. In short, traditional cost accounting is narrow-minded.

Managers and accountants accustomed to the old system may balk at this, but ask why they need to know the cost of making an individual product or service and you will most likely get some combination of three answers: to determine the selling price, to reduce costs and to value inventory. The fact is, however, that except for government cost-plus contracts or where a monopoly exists, the market determines the selling price—not the accountant. Regarding cost reduction, any business should be concentrating on reducing costs for the entire enterprise, not for individual products. And there are alternate methods for inventory valuation in a lean environment.

In the end, every enterprise is trying to profitably use its resources to provide customers with products or services that are competitive in terms of cost, quality and delivery. In his book *Kaizen*, Masaaki Imai describes it this way:

> "The ultimate goal of a company is to make profits. Assuming this is self-evident, the next 'superordinate' goals of the company should be such cross-functional goals as quality, cost, and scheduling (quantity and delivery). Without achieving these goals, the company will be left behind by the competition because of inferior quality, will find its profits eroded by higher costs, and will be unable to deliver the products in time for the customer. If these cross-functional goals are realized, profits will follow. Therefore, we should regard all the other management functions as existing to serve the three superordinate goals of QCS (Quality, Cost, and Scheduling)."

The formula for determining the cost of a product was once simple. When standard cost accounting was established, the typical manufacturer's cost of production was approximately 30 percent material content, 60 percent touch labor, and 10 percent overhead. In that environment, the practice of allocating overhead as a function of touch labor was legitimate and did not create significant distortions in determining product costs. Today the typical manufacturer probably has a cost structure that is more like 60 percent material content, 10 percent touch labor and 30 percent overhead. This shift from higher direct cost to higher indirect cost is principally the result of automation and its corresponding larger capital equipment component. Consequently, using traditional allocation methods leads to potentially significant distortion in calculating product cost.

In a lean environment, a second noticeable change will be the drop in inventory levels. As a company becomes more comfortable with just-in-time methods of doing business, all types of inventory—including work-in-process, raw materials and finished goods—will decrease as annual stock turns increase to 15 or 20 or more turns per year. This gives accountants the opportunity to reassess the process of valuing inventory for GAAP purposes.

Leaders who practice cost management will also find their attention turning to issues like product design. In most organizations, there is an appalling lack of valid information flowing between people in marketing, product design and process engineering. The results are products designed without customer input and that do not consider manufacturing's needs or limitations. This means that many new products are put into production with designs that are hard to make, creating production inefficiencies and failing to achieve desired profit levels.

To fully explore the implications of cost accounting versus cost management—which requires moving from a micro to a macro level of oversight—we need to break the subject down into three components: cost planning, cost control and cost accounting.

Cost Planning

The concept of cost planning focuses on how to design products and processes that will yield the lowest costs while meeting customer requirements. Most studies on the subject of cost planning reveal that somewhere between 80 and 95 percent of the life-cycle cost of a product is committed during the design process. That means that only 5-20 percent of the total cost is susceptible to future cost reduction efforts without redesigning the product.

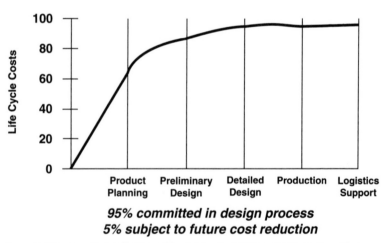

95% committed in design process
5% subject to future cost reduction

Source: Cost Management for TodayÖs Advanced Manufacturing-The CAM-I Conceptual Design, Harvard Business School Press, 1988

Figure 5.1 When the Life-Cycle Costs of a Product are Committed to by a Business

Figure 5.1 shows when life-cycle costs are committed to by the business. Figure 5.2 demonstrates the conflict that exists between when costs are committed versus when they occur and are recognized by the accounting system. It is easy to lose sight of the life cycle cost implications of design decisions without a conscious effort because the accounting systems do not report them until incurred. It is in the cost planning stage that this conscious effort is made.

Historically, Wiremold had long product development cycle times. Like many manufacturing companies, product development was often measured in years. In the early 1990s they adopted the product development process know as Quality Function Deployment, or QFD, which can be described as getting the voice of the customer into the product development

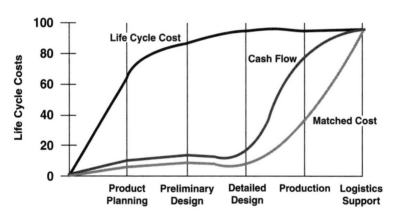

Low cash outlay in the product planning and design phases disguise the impact on total product costs

Source: Cost Management for TodayÖs Advanced Manufacturing-The CAM-I Conceptual Design, Harvard Business School Press, 1988

Figure 5.2 The Conflict in Product Costs: When They are Committed, Versus When They Occur and When They are Recognized by Accounting

process. Using QFD, Wiremold sought to introduce products to the market that satisfy real customer needs. Through an organized methodology of identifying customer needs and evaluating each of them on product design, more effort is expended in the product definition stage of the process in order to reduce the amount of redesign—otherwise known as waste—that generally occurs at the back end of most processes. Figure 5.3 demonstrates this principal. Using QFD, Wiremold has been able to significantly reduce the development cycle time and increase the number of new products that customers actually want. Shortly after QFD was introduced, the concept of Target Costing was integrated into the equation.

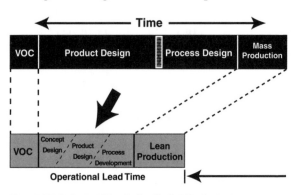

Figure 5.3 Reducing Lead Time for New Product Development

Traditionally, product development has involved engineers working in separate cubicles, rarely discussing their ideas with other departments, and then simply tossing the design over the wall to the next department when finished. Marketing would describe the product required, product engineers designed it and then manufacturing tried to make it. Only when the product was ready to launch was the cost calculated. If the cost was too high, the product was either redesigned or the company settled for a lower profit. Or the product was abandoned. However, there is a better way.

Target Costing is defined by Michihaur Sakurai, professor of accounting at Tokyo's Senshu University, as: "A cost-planning tool used for controlling design specifications and production techniques. Therefore, it is oriented much more towards management and engineering than towards accounting. A successful implementation of target costing requires the use of value engineering and other cost engineering tools."

At its core, Target Costing simply recognizes the economic fact that we have long since passed from an environment where Cost + Profit = Selling Price. Now, Selling Price—Cost = Profit. For most companies, selling prices are set by the market and profit is determined by how cost effective we can be. Target Costing forces this recognition by requiring that the selling price be determined at the beginning of the product development process and a desired profit, which is set by management, is subtracted in order to determine a cost target. By making this cost target one of the elements of the product specification, products can be designed to meet both external (customer) and internal (profit) needs. But the only way this can be achieved is to have a cross-functional product development team, involving associates from engineering, marketing, manufacturing and accounting. Not every member needs to be involved at every step in the process, but all need to have input.

As indicated by Mr. Sakurai, the development process must include both product and process development. The concurrent design of both product and process, sometimes called Design for Manufacturability, is the most effective way to reduce the amount of life cycle cost that is committed during the product design phase.

Cost Control

In a traditional manufacturing environment, an attempt is made at cost control using standard cost and variance analysis. Many companies have armies of cost accountants poring over variance reports after month end, trying to determine the reason for variances. The problem is that, except for those companies that exercise lot identification—as in the pharmaceutical industry—it is virtually impossible to trace an unfavorable variance to its root cause. If a manufacturing order is closed out during the first week of a month, and unfavorable labor variances are reported after the end of the month, how do you know what conditions existed at the time the variance was created? Do you know what day the product was made, what shift, by which operators using which machines? The likelihood of any real remedial action being identified by variance analysis is virtually zero.

The role of cost control in a lean environment is to reduce cost by eliminating waste. When information is presented to management that contains a significant level of allocated cost, not much corrective action can be taken to reduce costs other than getting it reallocated to someone else. Therefore, it is important to think in terms of presenting information that minimizes and segregates allocated costs. Allocating overhead to an individual machine is not informative. Understanding why one product line requires twice as much purchasing effort is actionable. One effective way of doing this is to move away from looking at profitability by individual product. Instead, look at profitability by groups or families of products. At this higher level, a better proportion of cost can be assigned versus allocated. This higher level of assigned costs increases accountability and the likelihood that real costs can be eliminated. (See Chapter 6 for more detail.)

In order to control costs, people need information that is timely and relevant, such as the performance measurements discussed in Chapter 3. Using those techniques will yield effective cost control because information will be timelier and more specific than a variance analysis could ever be.

Cost Accounting

Traditional cost accounting is dependant on establishing a standard cost for every product and every component that a company makes. This standard cost is comprised of material, direct labor and allocated overhead. The material portion is derived from a Bill of Material, which contains a quantity for each element used to make the product. It is, in effect, a recipe. Each element is then valued using a standard unit price. One would think that this would be straightforward and yield clear results. However, different companies use different methods of calculating this.

Some companies only note the quantities called for by engineering specifications. But others build in an allowable scrap, or yield, factor. Regarding the unit price, some use the current price and some use a forecasted price. The determination of the direct labor portion, as called for in the Routing (the how-to portion of the recipe) is subject to similar variations. Some companies define the amount of labor required as the optimum time. Others use the average time and still others build in safety factors just to avoid future unfavorable variances. We know of one company that used a piecework pay system and its direct labor standards were negotiated with the union since the standards affected workers' pay. The standards were very lenient. Some companies treat setup time as a direct labor operation, thereby driving bigger batches in order to reduce the reported unit cost, while others treat it as overhead. Overhead is usually allocated on the basis of methods devised decades ago when overhead, or indirect costs, was minimal. Using those same methods today yields inaccurate allocations, at best.

The cumulative effect of these problems with setting standard costs is poor decision making. How many times have we seen companies promote products based on perceived profitability or discontinue products because of perceived lack of profitability? The reality is that most companies do not know their product costs, but think they do. Executives think they know the costs out to the fourth decimal place. We receive computer reports that show very precise costs, catalogue number by catalogue number, and lose sight of the fact that much of the cost has been allocated and contains safety factors. Therefore, it is just an estimate. And because of the significant change in the cost elements over time, the allocation of overhead based on hours has resulted in significant distortions in reported cost.

Even though the traditional standard cost system results in inaccurate cost estimates, this is not the worst of it. Most people cannot understand the Profit and Loss financial statement generated by standard cost practices. It presents sales, standard costs and standard gross margin in a way that implies what the margin would be if standards were achieved, and then proceeds to add or deduct up to six to eight variances that people don't really understand. The six variances generally used are material price and usage, labor rate and efficiency, and overhead spending and volume. Two other overhead variances—excess capacity and efficiency—are sometimes used also. (See sidebar for discussion of the use of capacity variances.)

Even though most people can't understand a standard cost P & L, they learn very quickly that unfavorable variances are bad and to be avoided. This can cause many types of dysfunctional behavior. For example, purchasing agents may negotiate price reductions and sacrifice quality. This may cause higher scrap rates, but that's not what purchasing agents are measured on. That's someone else's issue.

One of the most significant dysfunctional behaviors that occurs in the attempt to avoid unfavorable overhead volume variances is that factories begin to create labor hours. This happens because people in the factory learn very quickly that hours absorb overhead and so creating hours is good. During the last week of the month, managers start looking to see what parts are on hand and what products can be made, in order to add labor hours to the final tab. But there is no linkage between what the customer wants and what the factory is making. As a result, unneeded inventory is created, occupying space and consuming working capital. This inventory is eventually sold at the end-of-quarter specials organized by marketing or written off as obsolete. In addition, this build up and sell off of unnecessary inventory contributes to the layoff-and-hire syndrome that exists in many businesses.

Many companies that have recognized the inaccuracies created by allocating overhead on the basis of labor or machine hours have turned instead to Activity Based Costing, or ABC. In the ABC model, costs are allocated based on *cost drivers*, which are defined as activities that give rise to costs. In Purchasing, for example, the driver might be the number of purchase orders issued. The cost of the purchasing activity would be allocated to products based on the number of purchase orders each generated. In this way, each element of overhead would be studied to identify its driver(s) and the cost allocated on that basis.

There are several problems with ABC. First, it is still an allocation method and wants estimates to be expressed in very precise terms. Second, it is expensive to establish and maintain. In an article in favor of ABC in *Business Week*, Hugh Filman wrote, "Even for big diversified companies, these programs may be too pricey to implement and maintain."[6] Mr. Filman then sites Jeffrey M. Aldridge of accounting firm Grant Thornton as saying a pilot project can cost from $100,000 to $500,000. Although Mr. Filman argues that there is a justifiable payback on this effort, we would dispute that.

In many cases, ABC may lead one to believe that the way to reduce costs is to produce in bigger batches. For example, if Purchasing overhead is allocated on the basis of the number of purchase orders issued, there is a motivation to buy in bigger lot sizes and reduce the number of purchasing transactions. Or if machine set-up time were allocated on the number of setups done, there is a motivation to reduce the number of setups by making larger batches. This is the opposite of lean manufacturing.

As previously noted, most companies don't know their product costs, but think they do—out to four decimal places. Most businesses do not have to maintain a data collection system to capture individual product costs on a continuous basis.

The amount of resources that are consumed by shop floor reporting systems, such as labor costs, do not contribute anything significant to the effort of reducing waste and can be

---

6 Business Week, August 7, 2000 page 86j

classified as waste itself. The amount of time needed to collect labor cost will increase dramatically as batch sizes are reduced. If it took two minutes to collect the data for a batch of 1,000, it still takes two minutes to collect the data for a batch of one. Eliminating these shop floor reporting systems and their related transactions represents a significant contribution to productivity improvement.

In addition, enough of the data being collected is wrong so as to make the final answer wrong. Accomplished manually, the collection of labor hours and units produced is bound to be rife with error. So, some companies spend huge amounts of resources to mechanize the system with bar codes and computers, resulting in a system that is almost—very nearly—accurate. When one considers the thousands or millions of transactions reported, it is clear that there are enough errors to distort the data. Second, most companies' labor reporting systems are independent of the time clock systems used to pay employees. In these instances, the two systems must be reconciled before payroll can be finalized. Generally, an honest effort is made to do this, but at the eleventh hour the labor-hour data is *plugged* to balance to the time clock system.

> Plugged (plugd): The insertion of whatever number is needed to balance reports.

We have never heard of a company not meeting a payday deadline because the two systems didn't reconcile. What would that do for employee morale?

The third reason the answer in the product cost column is wrong is because in many cases inappropriate allocation methods are used. Many of the methods were established long ago and, as companies' operations changed, allocation methods did not. In addition, there may be more than one acceptable method of allocation that could yield significantly different results. Thus, that precise-to-the-fourth-digit product cost that you are looking at is merely the result of a choice of allocation methods, even if all of the input data were correct. Choosing a different but acceptable method gives a different cost.

Given the fact that individual product costs are based on partially inaccurate data and subjective allocation methods, one should be cautious in making decisions based on this information. However, there are instances where a company does need to have a reasonable idea of its product cost. Since product costs do not—or should not—vary greatly from day to day, product costs can be calculated as needed instead of spending money on a formal cost system. This approach of calculating cost on an ad hoc basis using actual costs will achieve a higher degree of accuracy, at a lower cost, than maintaining the traditional cost-data collection systems.

The elements of a product's cost can be defined as the sum of material cost, assigned processing or conversion cost and allocated cost. Material cost is relatively easy to obtain by referring to the products' Bill of Materials and the company's purchasing records for purchase prices. However, scrap factors should not be added since scrap is waste and needs to be eliminated. If, during the implementation of lean, the manufacturing process is reorganized into product families, a high degree of processing costs can be directly assigned because product-specific work cells are created. In fact, it is possible to get to a point where not much more than occupancy costs are allocated to the product families. Some, but probably not many, companies may be able to group products into families where the cycle times for all of the products are within a very narrow band. In this case, the total processing and occupancy costs for the family can be divided by the number of units produced. When this average cost is added to the specific product material cost, a total approximate cost can be obtained without significant distortion.

Most companies have product families with significantly differing cycle times, so the average-cost method described above will not be adequate. Some companies have used Activity-Based Costing (ABC) as a substitute for traditional standard costing. In ABC, costs are allocated on the basis of cost drivers (e.g., number of purchase orders issued). Many companies have found that ABC encourages larger batches in order to spread the cost over a larger number of units, thereby "reducing" the cost per unit. In lean, the thrust is to reduce or eliminate the cost, not just spread it over more widgets. Because ABC is highly dependant on allocations, we do not see this as a desirable alternative.

One of the basic principles of performance measurement is to motivate the right decisions, as we said in Chapter 3. The same could be said of product costing methods. Accordingly, a third method that could be employed is to allocate processing and occupancy costs based on product lead times. Lead time is defined in a broad sense: process time plus inspection time plus move time plus wait time. Inspection, move and wait time are all non-value added, or waste. Thus, as a process is improved and the lead time reduced (i.e., waste is eliminated), the product cost will be lower.

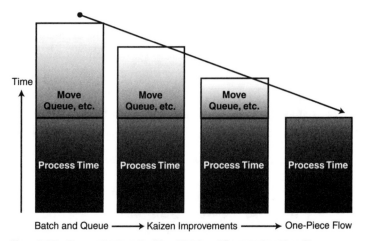

Figure 5.4 The Progression From Traditional Batch and Queue to One-Piece Flow

Figure 5.4 illustrates the progression from a traditional batch and queue environment to a pure flow, just-in-time process. Figure 5.5 illustrates the difference between the results of standard cost and lead-time cost for two products. In this case a standard cost system shows that product A has a lower conversion costs since the total standard time is lower. However, if costs are attached to products on the basis of lead time, product B has the lower reported costs. In addition, as the process is improved and lead time is reduced (i.e., velocity increased), the reported cost of the products would decrease.

	Product A				Product B			
Process	#1	#2	#3	Total	#1	#2	#3	Total
Standard Time	2	10	3	15	7	5	8	20
Lead Time	10	10	10	30	8	8	8	24

Standard Time Shows Product A Has Lowest Cost
Lead Time Shows Product B Has Lowest Cost

Figure 5.5 In This Illustration, We See How Standard Time Hides Waste and Ignores Bottlenecks

In all of these cases, cost is not absolute, but merely an estimate that is dependant upon the allocation method chosen. It is important that management clearly understands this; otherwise, decisions about which products to sell, or not to sell, could be made for the wrong reasons. It is much more important that management understands the profitability of a portfolio of related products. The apparently low-margin products that fill out the line will become acceptable if they provide a competitive advantage in the eyes of the customer and the product line as a whole generates an acceptable profit.

Tell a traditional accountant that detailed product costs need not be maintained, however, and the argument comes back that those numbers *are* needed to satisfy the auditors who want to know inventory values. But let's look at the standard "clean opinion" that auditors give out:

"We conduct our audits in accordance with generally accepted auditing standards. Those standards require that we plan and perform the audit to obtain reasonable assurance about whether the financial statements are free of material misstatement. An audit includes examining, on a test basis, evidence supporting the amounts and disclosures in the financial statements. An audit also includes assessing the accounting principles used and significant estimates made by management, as well as evaluating the overall financial statement presentation. ... In our opinion, the consolidated financial statements referred to above present fairly, in all material respects, the consolidated financial position of ... "

Note the key phrases "free of material misstatement ... assessing significant estimates," and "presents fairly, in all material respects." These phrases acknowledge that items in the financial statements are based on estimates, including the valuation of inventory, and that the financial statements are fair in all significant respects, giving recognition to the materiality principle.

If a company turns its inventory two or three times, which is not unusual for a traditional batch and queue company, it will have four to six months inventory on hand. This represents a significant balance-sheet item, and a small error in valuation can have a significant effect on reported income. Therefore, the typical audit devotes a considerable amount of time testing the methods used to allocate costs to the inventory, in addition to obsolescence and net-realizable-value tests.

On the other hand, it is not unusual for a good just-in-time company to turn its work-in-process and finished goods inventory 25 to 50 times a year. In other words, these companies would have only one or two weeks of inventory on hand that has incurred any processing time, and therefore need to have labor and overhead allocated to it. It is relatively easy to calculate, at a macro level, one or two weeks of labor and overhead, and to capitalize this amount via an accounting journal entry at the end of each month. And even if this estimate were wrong by a full week, it would not create a significant misstatement of the financial statement.

In addition, when inventories are kept this low, the risk of obsolescence is reduced and the net realizable value of the inventory taken as a whole is not an issue. In our experience, using this method is not only acceptable to auditors, it also reduces the time and cost of the audit. Thus the argument that unit costs are needed to value inventory is not valid in a lean environment.

Making the Transition

The historical obsession with determining the cost of individual products consumes enormous resources and diverts us from the task of driving real cost down. However, eliminating a standard cost system and all of its related transactions is not easy and can't be done overnight. Many of the transactions that supply data to the cost system also supply data to the MRP operating system. Consequently, transactions such as labor tickets and move tickets cannot be discontinued until alternate operating processes are implemented. There must be a coordinated effort between the operations and accounting to accomplish this.

As production cells are configured and flow production is implemented, manufacturing routings can be flattened or eliminated and labor tickets can be reduced and finally eradicated. As kanban systems are implemented, move tickets can be eliminated. When a company makes serious progress in its transition to lean manufacturing, and no attempt is made to eliminate these redundant transactions, a serious disconnect occurs between operations and accounting. Eventually operations will realize they are processing the transactions only for accounting, since they now have alternate processes to satisfy their needs, and the integrity of the data being reported becomes even more suspect. Nobody wants to produce numbers just for the sake of producing numbers.

USE OF CAPACITY VARIANCE

Cost accountants apply a variety of techniques in setting overhead rates in a standard cost system. Sometimes the rates are set plant-wide so that there is one rate applied to all products. Sometimes the rates are set by department or some other segmentation, so that different rates are applied to different products. In all cases, the rate generally represents budgeted overhead costs divided by some number of hours. The number of hours is typically based on the budgeted hours necessary to support the sales forecast.

However, some companies will set the overhead rates using theoretical capacity—the number of hours that would be consumed if the plant were operating at full capacity. This produces the lowest possible overhead rate for the plant and therefore the lowest standard cost. If this method is used and the number of expected hours based on current sales levels is less than the theoretical capacity, an unfavorable capacity variance is guaranteed. When companies use this method of setting overhead rates, this capacity variance is typically reported separately in the profit and loss statement, due to unabsorbed overhead associated with the unused capacity.

In addition, volume variances are also reported and represent the unabsorbed overhead when actual hours are less than budgeted hours. We have seen instances when the overhead rate was based on theoretical capacity, but

▶

the entire unabsorbed overhead was calculated as merely a volume variance. In these cases, up to 50 percent of the standard gross margin was consumed by unfavorable variances and the financial people used this to beat up the sales and marketing people for hurting profits by not generating enough sales volume. This in turn encourages the sales people to try to generate additional volume at any price. In fact, the real problem was that the financial people approved large capital investments that were justified on a lower unit cost, which was based on high throughput. However, during the approval process, nobody seriously challenged whether that level of throughput—or sales—was possible for the business in any reasonable time.

6

PLAIN ENGLISH MANAGEMENT FINANCIAL STATEMENTS

THE AVERAGE RECIPIENT OF A STANDARD cost-based profit and loss statement does not understand the document in his hands. It communicates nothing. Worse still, for those few that do understand it, these statements fail to give meaningful information about what is really happening in the operation. To remedy this situation, we have developed management financial statements presented in plain language. This chapter illustrates a step-by-step method for creating these statements.

Look at a typical standard cost Profit and Loss statement though the gross profit line (Figure 6.1). In this example, sales increased from one period to another, but gross profit did not. It stayed flat in absolute dollars and declined as a percentage of sales. If a

REAL NUMBERS

business manager were to receive this financial statement after the end of the period, where should he look to make corrective actions to insure that future increased sales actually result in higher profits?

In 6.1, standard cost as a percentage of sales remained at 50 percent of sales. Assuming no significant product mix change, it could be assumed that the standards were not changed to anticipate any process improvements.

	This Year	Last Year
Net Sales	100,000	90,000
Cost of Sales:		
Standard Cost	48,000	45,000
Purchase Price Variance	(3,000)	10,000
Material Usage Variance	(2,000)	5,000
Labor Efficiency Variance	7,000	(8,000)
Labor Rate Variance	(2,000)	9,000
Overhead Volume Variance	2,000	2,000
Overhead Spending Variance	(2,000)	8,000
Overhead Efficiency Variance	16,000	(17,000)
Total Cost of Sales	64,000	54,000
Gross Profit	36,000	36,000
Gross Profit %	36.0%	40.0%

Figure 6.1 Standard Cost Profit and Loss Statement

Also, purchase price variance went from $1,000 unfavorable to $1,000 favorable. Does this mean that the purchasing department has done a good job negotiating with vendors? If so, did they negotiate a lower price but sacrifice quality or delivery? Or does it mean that the purchasing department did a good job negotiating with the cost accountants in setting the new standards? This is not uncommon when material standards are based on anticipated prices rather than current actual prices.

The only clear statement made by Figure 6.1 is that the change in each of the variances raised more questions than the financial statement can provide answers to. The business manager cannot really tell why profits did not increase even though sales did. As Wiremold made the transition to lean, it became quickly obvious that they needed to give operating associates better financial information. As a starting point for developing an alternative to standard cost-based Profit & Loss statements, Orry and his team established several principles to which the new financial statement must adhere:

- ❑ Useable by non-accountants
- ❑ Eliminates complexity in presentation
- ❑ Has higher assignable costs, lower allocated costs
- ❑ Includes both financial and non-financial information
- ❑ Motivates the right decisions
- ❑ Complies with GAAP principles

The objective of making the management financial statements accessible to non-accountants seems obvious since most of the users are not accountants. But the objective is rarely realized. Management reporting is a major product of the financial organization and if users do not understand those reports then all of the effort that goes into producing them can be classified as waste. An accountant must develop the eyes of an outsider. Keep in mind that what you're really doing is developing a new product and, in order to create something desirable, you need to get the customer's feedback into the process.

One way to make financial statements more understandable is to eliminate the complexity of presentation. The statements in

Figure 6.1 present the financial results in a manner so complex that no meaningful conclusions about the state of the operations can be made. We recommend reducing the level of allocated costs in order to increase personal responsibility and accountability. Assigned costs are directly incurred; allocated costs are indirect and examples might include: depreciation of the building, property taxes and insurance as borne by each of the company's product lines. Using allocated costs, managers are tempted to make operating results look good by changing allocation methods. Looking at results that are based on costs incurred by, and therefore assigned to an operation, increases accountability. Allocated costs should be separated from those that are assigned. The way we improve results is by eliminating waste, not shifting blame.

Along with these columns of dollar figures, non-financial measurements are also needed to track the physical factors of a business, because improving productivity requires physical change. Accordingly, a comprehensive set of management reports must include both financial and non-financial data in order to provide a more complete understanding of the business. These measures could include the number of days of inventory on hand, customer service measurements, number of days in outstanding accounts receivable, key productivity measures and defect reduction, to name a few. The results of presenting financial information in a clear, understandable manner, combined with key non-financial metrics should improve the organization's ability to motivate the right decisions.

For instance, clarity in the metrics will ensure that the products being produced are the ones customers want, not the ones creating the most absorption hours. We know that, in an attempt to avoid unfavorable overhead volume variances, managers routinely

increase labor hours in order to improve overhead absorption—
no matter the effect on inventory or productivity (see Chapter
5). This behavior may make the currently reported profits look
better, but it consumes cash, space and other resources by
increasing inventory. If volume doesn't increase in the short
term, increasing labor hours merely postpones the day of reck-
oning, particularly in the high-tech industry, where short product life cycles increase the possibility of future write-offs for
obsolete inventory. In other words, the method of reporting
financial information has caused dysfunctional behavior. Finally,
nothing should be done to violate GAAP; we are not talking
about changing accounting principles, but about presenting
financial information in a clear and understandable fashion.

Now take the same company and rewrite their financial report
as in Figure 6.2. It is a simple presentation—even elementary—
but it gives a clear picture of the prime costs of the business:
material, labor and overhead. The labor and overhead are segre-
gated into processing costs and occupancy costs. This is helpful
when Profit & Loss statements are produced for each product
family within the business. Processing costs are assigned to the
product family and occupancy costs are allocated and represent
a small portion of the total costs.

Factory salaries for management and support personnel such as
manufacturing engineers and purchasing are up by five percent.
As managers of this business we know what the average wage
increase has been and, combined with the knowledge that some
manufacturing engineers were added to facilitate process
improvement, we can conclude that five percent is reasonable.
Benefits are up 40 percent so we know we should talk to HR
about causes and possible corrective actions.

	This Year	Last Year	+(-) %
Net Sales	100,000	90,000	11.1
Cost of Sales:			
Purchases	25,300	34,900	
Inventory material: (increase) decrease	6,000	(6,000)	
Total Material Costs	31,300	28,900	8.3
Processing Costs:			
Factory Wages	11,000	11,500	(4.3)
Factory Salaries	2,100	2,000	5.0
Factory Benefits	7,000	5,000	40.0
Services and Supplies	2,200	2,500	(12.0)
Equipment Depreciation	2,000	1,900	5.3
Scrap	2,000	4,000	(50.0)
Total Processing Costs	26,300	26,900	(2.2)
Occupancy Costs:			
Building Depreciation	200	200	0.0
Building Services	2,200	2,000	10.0
Total Occupancy Costs:	2,400	2,200	9.1
Total Manufacturing Costs	60,000	58,000	3.4
Inventory-labor, Overhead (increase) decrease	4,000	(4,000)	
Cost of Sales	64,000	54,000	18.5
Gross Profit	36,000	36,000	0.0
Gross Profit %	36.0%	40.0%	

Figure 6.2 An Alternative Presentation

Services and supplies—true overhead items—are under control and the increase in depreciation appears to be reasonable in light of capital spending. Scrap is down 50 percent, indicating that quality is improving. In the area of occupancy costs, building services are up more than expected, but we also know that energy costs have increased significantly this year and represent the major cause.

And yet, even though sales are up more that 11 percent, gross profit is flat. What would have been a mystery in the older style report is quickly identified here: the company was building inventory last year and liquidating it this year. Last year we capitalized operating costs in inventory and this year we must charge it to operating results as that inventory is sold. This presentation recognizes the fact that the balance-sheet asset that we call "inventory" is comprised of two things. The first is the material content—the real asset. The second is deferred labor and overhead. Under the matching principle discussed in Chapter 2, labor and overhead incurred to build product that is not sold in the current period must be capitalized. It is then expensed during the period in which the product is sold. In other words, in years when inventory is increased, that period's profits are enhanced by moving costs out of the profit and loss statement and onto the balance sheet. Conversely, in years when inventory is decreased, which happens rapidly during the lean transformation, those periods are penalized by having to recognize this charge for past years' expenses in addition to the current ones. In fact, the factory was doing the right things, reducing costs, improving inventory turns and generating cash, but the standard cost financial statements hid this.

This is why many operating people who begin to have some success with their lean transformation might wrestle with managers who do not have a clear understanding of its implications on the financial statement and the cash-flow report. Managers who still use standard cost-based financial statements say, "I don't know what you're doing, but whatever it is, stop it. You're killing profits."

In this example, if we assume that the factory associates received a 3 percent wage increase, then the number of hours incurred would have been reduced by approximately 7.3 percent (+ 3.0 percentage rate—7.3% hours = - 4.3 percent). If we also assume that the sales increase was all volume (i.e. no price increases and no significant mix change), and that approximately 26 percent of the total sales were satisfied through inventory sell-off, then one could argue that there was a productivity loss. The total production was down approximately 37 percent as follows:

	Last Year	This Year	Percentage Change
Sales	90,000	100,000	+11.1%
Inventory Change at Selling Price*	26,300	(26,300)	
Production at Selling Price	116,300	73,300	-36.6%

(*10,000 inventory change at an average of 38 percent gross profit)

Now, let's keep in mind that significant productivity gains cannot be achieved without full participation of the workforce. Since people will not willingly work themselves out of a job, companies that are committed to achieving these levels of improvement must guarantee that no one will lose employment because of productivity gains. In the example given above, the reduction in hours was achieved by reduced overtime and attrition. The excess labor hours, temporarily created by the inventory reduction, were devoted to training and kaizen activities. Using layoffs to avoid this cost is not acceptable because once the inventory is reduced to the desired level, those labor hours (i.e. people) will be needed to satisfy current customer demand.

Unfortunately, in the quest for short-term gains, companies use layoffs extensively when productivity improves. In doing, so they reduce the probability of any meaningful cooperation of the workforce to achieve significant future productivity gains.

People just won't willingly work themselves out of a job. Management must take a longer-term view and put meaning into the phase "our people are our most important asset." As time goes on and productivity gains continue to be achieved, it is acceptable to ensure that, as attrition takes place, it is difficult for replacements to be hired. In this way, the productivity gains will translate into higher profits.

We do recognize that the employment guarantee can be a difficult commitment for CEOs. But we also know this: The reluctance to ensure employment is a major barrier to successfully implementing lean, and amounts to an admission by senior managers that they cannot grow the business fast enough to absorb significant productivity gains.

Once we have made the transition to a set of management reports that contains both financial and non-financial information in a format that non-accountants can understand, what do we do with it? The obvious conclusion is that you can make the information more widely available, since more people can understand it. In turn, as more people understand it and see the results of their efforts clearly reflected over time, a more productive and profitable behavior will be motivated. Companies that want to move to open book management, as described in Chapter 2, will have a financial tool that facilitates this.

Changing something as fundamental as management's financial statements is easier to say than to do. Your colleagues have spent years attempting to react to that old information, presented in a specific format. Taking that away—no matter how useless it was—may be politically difficult. Although many people may not realize it, the lower reporting levels of standard cost systems contain all of the data required to easily present a financial statement similar to the one in Figure 6.2.

At Wiremold, management reports were switched out in a manner so straightforward, it was almost sneaky. When new reports were ready, the traditional management reports were sent out first. About a week later, Orry distributed the alternate presentation, prepared off-line in a spreadsheet, with a note attached stating, "We're trying something new. Would love your feedback."

Two things happened. First, Orry's team received some useful feedback that improved their presentation, and gave them some buy-in from colleagues making the suggestions. As time went by and they continued to distribute the older reports a week before the new one, Accounting began getting calls as soon as managers received the traditional package. They asked for the alternate presentation sooner, and in place of the traditional presentation.

Mission accomplished.

WHERE TO FIND THE DATA

Even the most standard of standard cost systems contains the data required to prepare a Plain English Management Financial Statement. If we trace each line item in the statement back to its source, we discover that the information we need is in the company's transactional systems and trial balance.

Sales, and the related items to get from *gross* to *net* are not a problem because they are reported in the same way

▶

Information about purchases, services and supplies come from the accounts payable system.

Wages and salary costs for the various categories come from the company's payroll system. Benefit costs come from a combination of the account payable system (e.g. health insurance premiums) or accounting journal entries (e.g. accrual of pension cost).

Depreciation comes from the fixed asset system. Scrap is derived from a shop floor system that captures the information about product that is scraped and sent to scrap recovery.

The item that can give some difficulty is the change in inventory. At the beginning, when inventory levels are still high, the difference in the value of the inventory as recorded in the perpetual inventory records at the beginning of the month and the end of the month is the source of this information. As inventory levels come down, alternative methods are possible. For example, at some companies that have achieved 20 or more inventory turns, almost the entire inventory (no nuts and bolts...remember accuracy vs. precision) can be counted at the end of the month within a few hours. This allows the company to eliminate its perpetual inventory system and all related transactions.

Operations uses kanban for its purposes and accounting uses a count for the financial statements. This inventory is valued as material content, with the labor and overhead content added via journal entry using the techniques described in Chapter 5.

▶

Other companies use a hybrid of these two methods. They maintain a perpetual inventory system, valued at material cost only, and add labor and overhead via journal entries. On a net basis, considerable waste is eliminated. Thus, even in a company that needs to continue to produce the standard cost financial statements for some period, the data exist within its financial systems to produce the Plain English Statements in parallel.

7

THE ONE-DAY CLOSE

IN JUST ABOUT EVERY ORGANIZATION, there are efforts to increase the velocity of change and speed products to the customer. E-commerce drives us toward immediate ordering and fulfillment. UPS can get a package to your door by 8 a.m. All-night access is expected at cash machines, grocery stores, gas stations. We want instant access to weather reports, stock quotes, bank balances—and we usually get it. But the poor financial statement is still in process days and even weeks after the end of the reporting period. At that point, can we even call it relevant?

If we want the organization to respect the information we offer and value its content, we cannot give it to them days after the activity is completed. And let's face it, in some cases that information is weeks late. In a lean environment, immediate visual feedback is available throughout the business. Anyone can walk past a cell or work group and see how many pieces have been produced, how many hours have been lost to unplanned downtime and what the customer is buying. Leadership can react to that information instantaneously. Then we show up two weeks later, offering a report of how much was shipped, what the costs were and how much money was made. Jean can recall many times that she personally delivered the financials to other executives and managers and was greeted warmly, but with distance. All of the polite words would be spoken: "How is your day? Here's your report. Oh, thank you very much. See you later." On leaving that office, though, she knew her report hit the round file or recycling bin quicker than the door swung shut. The problem was, she had just delivered old news. What do you do with old news? Wrap up the trash. Use it for the birdcage.

Let's think about the cost of a financial statement. Better yet, let's figure the cost of a financial statement using a chart like Figure 7.1. Calculate the number of people in the accounting team who work on closing the books. Write down their names and ask them which day they start to work on closing. Call it day one or day two or whatever. Then write down the day that the financial report is published—say, day seven. Calculate the number of days per person and then add it up.

This reveals the total days spent on creating a financial statement. Now add in your employees' salaries. How much does it cost? You can even use an average salary and apply it to everyone. This can be a good barometer for those who chose to start cutting down days for closing. Once you see how much those reports cost, you can see the value in reducing time spent on their creation.

	Starting Day	Closing Day	# of Days Closing	Salary**	Cost/Day	Total Cost to Close
Rosalie	2	10	8	$50,000	$192.31	$1,538
Linda	3	10	7	$50,000	$192.31	$1,346
Robert	4	10	6	$50,000	$192.31	$1,154
Cathy	1	10	9	$50,000	$192.31	$1,731
Becky	1	10	9	$50,000	$192.31	$1,731
Sandy	1	10	9	$50,000	$192.31	$1,731
Janis	3	10	7	$50,000	$192.31	$1,346
Jean	7	10	3	$50,000	$192.31	$577
Patti	6	10	4	$50,000	$192.31	$769
Barbara	3	10	7	$50,000	$192.31	$1,346

Total Cost in Days Dollars for One Month	69	
		$13,269
Total Cost in Days Dollars for 12 Months	828	
		$159,231

Total Days in a Year	260
Number of People	10
Total Available Days in a Year	2600
Total Days Spent on Financials	828
% of Time Spent on Financials	32%

** You could put in the actual salaries of each person, but in the interest of accuracy (instead of precision) we just used an average.

Figure 7.1 Calculate the Cost of Your Financial Statements

Most companies would probably agree that financial statements are vital to the company. Therefore we want to rush them to our colleagues as quickly as possible. They have a short shelf life, maybe just days, so we cannot waste any time getting these perishable products to the customer. Look back at the cost of that statement. Was that more than you were willing to spend on out-of-date information?

There are two ways to attack the problem: Reduce the number of days that each person works on financials, then reduce the number of people involved in closing. We are not suggesting a reduction in the accounting staff, although that may be possible if your systems contain more waste than average. As illustrated in the Performance Measures chapter, there is plenty of valuable work for them, once the triangles are turned upside down.

Do not expect to cut out the number of days required for closing all at one time. Instead create and communicate a big vision: "We will achieve an Everyday Close." Then set interim targets. The first goal might be reducing the closing time by three days in the first quarter and taking two days out of closing in quarter two. Or decide to decrease the number of people involved with closing from eight down to five in three months. **WORM** your goals; make them **W**ritten, **O**bservable, **R**ealistic and **M**easurable.

Now, let's go looking for paths to meeting the target.

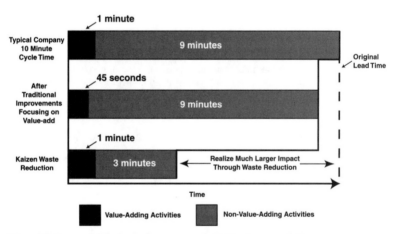

Figure 7.2 Companies Typically Concentrate on Making Incremental Improvements to the Value-Adding Process, Instead of Attacking Waste

Key Components

A key principle in lean is always the elimination of non-value added activities. In most companies it is easy to find the non-value added activities—such as moving around materials, extraneous bookkeeping, wasted motions—because non-value added can be 90 percent of the activity (Figure 7.2).

Traditionally, businesses have focused on reducing the amount of time it takes to do the value-added work. But if you first target the elimination or reduction of non-value-added work, the overall results are better, are achieved more quickly and morale is increased. No one wants to do work that is perceived as non-value added. Reducing the amount of time it takes to do value-added work can follow.

At Lantech, when Jean first started looking hard at the journal entries made after the end of the month, she found an amazing fact: the highest number of entries were posted to correct items from the prior month that had been coded to the wrong account. So the first transaction, which was wrong, required a second transaction to correct it, without any understanding being gleaned from the mistake. Lantech does not do that anymore. Now, when an accountant finds an incorrect entry, she does not merely correct it; she investigates why it was recorded incorrectly the first time.

These are usually great training opportunities. Occasionally, the team discovers that the process upstream was programmed to put the entry to the wrong account. The idea is to make your clerks into detectives, searching out how to get the data entered correctly at the source.

Another discovery at Lantech was particularly disheartening. When Jean looked at the smallest dollar items—all the nickel and dime transactions—they made up the largest number of entries on her books. About 80 percent of the entries were for just 20 percent of the total value. Sometimes that ratio was worse. Let's face it, in just about every company, entries are sometimes made for amounts that just don't matter. Frequently these entries are corrections of other entries, which add redundancy to irrelevancy. The rule now at Lantech is, if the amounts are small and do need to be fixed, let them be fixed in the following month. Small amounts do not influence decisions—remember the materiality principle—and so do not need to take up precious time that we need in order to rush our reports to the customer.

Here's another key principle for a fast close: Out of the Closing Window or, simply, Out of the Window. Let's say a number of the non-value-added steps have already been eliminated and you are left with a number of tasks that must be done, such as calculating warranty reserves and bonus reserves and creating an accrual for unpaid days worked. These essential-but-not-urgent items are sitting there, aimed at your most precious window.

Think of the closing window as the smallest opening in your house. There are a lot of bulky items that must pass through the house, on a deadline. Why would we try to shove everything through that one small opening? Instead, find a way to do the work *before* the end of the month. Think of set-up reduction work on the shop floor: all activities are divided into that which can be done while the machine is still running—external setup—and that which can only be done while the machine is at rest—the internal setup. In the monthly closing process, depreciation can be entered before the end of the month but income taxes cannot.

There are two main methods for identifying items that can be moved out of the closing window, and most lean organizations will probably end up using both. One is to do the work as it happens, eliminating all batch activities. The other method is to look closely to see when each piece of information is available and put it in your books at the first available moment.

At Lantech, as at about 80 percent of companies, a payroll service is used. A clerk—or an automatic system, at some companies—enters data three or four days in advance of payday. Summary reports and paychecks arrive a day before envelopes are handed out at Lantech. The summaries include dollar paid by department, taxes paid, vacation time versus regular time and overtime.

In the past, a Lantech accountant then dutifully entered this in the general ledger. She began on day two of the closing window and took about a day to complete her work, once numbers were reconfigured (allocating pay between two departments, etc). Jean investigated and asked: why not enter the summaries into the general ledger as soon as the information became available? That would remove payroll from the closing window altogether. Later, a team discovered that the payroll service could give Lantech an electronic version of the summaries, eliminating the need for re-entry. Now they get electronic files each week. A manual step in the process has been eliminated, and a task is removed from the closing window, bringing Lantech closer to real-time information.

Receiving and applying information weekly would have been such a huge task in a manual process that Jean would never have committed the time. But with all the waste eliminated in a hands-off process, she can get information that is basically free of effort—which is very lean. Accountants can now see payroll throughout the month, and are alerted to any problems or trends that can be addressed as they happen. It is much easier to diagnose problems as they happen rather than waiting until the end of a period where you wade through a sea of transactions, looking for an answer.

How about more complex issues? Warranty Reserves, for instance, is one of those tricky accounts that can consume vast amounts of time and add very little in terms of increased understanding of the company and product performance. Why is it so different than any other cost? It seems simple at first blush. There is a customer who has a product that breaks. The customer knows the product has, say, a one-year parts warranty. So, he contacts the manufacturer, who agrees to replace or repair the item. The maker spends some money doing this, of course. Why would the tracking of these numbers become so difficult?

A number of other areas share these complexities. There is not one solution to reducing the time and effort it takes to deal with the more complex accounts. The following describes a wide array of issues we discovered when dealing with warranties and the approaches we used to become lean. Eventually, after trying various techniques, we realized that the reserve—like other complex issues—is really just a guess of a good estimate.

Let's go back to the principle of Matching, which says that any significant cost must be included as an expense as soon as the cost is realized. So when a product covered by warranty is shipped and you know, based on prior experience, this product or a similar type of product has a measurable failure rate, then you must show the projected warranty expense for that item when it is shipped. Just by shipping it, you have accepted a reasonable expectation that warranty costs will be incurred in future. The tricky part is figuring out how much to expense.

The solution to booking warranty can vary depending on how large (or material) the warranty cost. Lantech was originally spending a lot of time trying to estimate this number and it was still just a guess because nobody knows which product will break, or what it will cost to fix the problem, until it actually happens.

Here are a couple of methods to try as you come to grips with warranty. By product line, define the actual warranty costs as a percentage of current sales. Perhaps look at your last year's historical results, but do not include your accrued costs, only the real costs. Let's call this the Warranty Percentage. Then, to calculate a simple accrual for the expected costs related to the products you ship this month, multiply that percentage by the current month's actual sales. This can be done inside the closing window. Or, to get it out of the closing window, take the total sales until the next-to-last day of the month and add in an estimate for the last day's sales; multiply that times the Warranty Percentage. Or if your information system allows for automated allocations, put the Warranty Percentage in and then let the warranty accrual be calculated automatically as part of the closing.

Over time, the percentage might change. Check it each quarter for fluctuations. If it does, try changing the percentage more or less frequently. Lantech found the percentage changed very slowly with a three-year warranty, so now they check every six months but only change it once a year.

Or perhaps sales are growing very fast and there is a worry that the historical relationship of warranty cost to current sales is inadequate. Then a different kind of relationship might be better. If the key message you hear is that figuring out which type of relationship to use is too complex, let the final application of that method be simple. Perhaps you have 100 products. You might do some complex analysis to discover the good rates to estimate cost. In the end, however, you might find there are only two levels of cost: high warranty costs that affect 10 products, and the lower warranties that the other 90 products fall into. In this case, we only need to use two simple rates to book the cost and we can do these calculations outside of the closing window.

Another alternative, if this cost is very significant for a company (remember materiality), might be to use a simple method for the first two months of a quarter and then get more precise after the third month. Try to find a simple method to make this guess, while ensuring that everyone is comfortable with the accuracy, conservatism and matching. If an acceptable reserve can be established using simplified methods, accountants can devote their time to something that adds value, like participating on a cross-functional team to determine the root causes of warranty claims in order to eliminate them. By reducing warranty claims to the point where they are immaterial, the discussion of warranty reserves is moot.

This example should give you an idea of how you might deal with other complex issues, such as depletion, software development capitalization, goodwill amortization and credit reserves.

On the path to a more lean accounting, we know that the time just after closing is a great opportunity to pull a team together and take a hard look at transactions. This is a time to reiterate the vision that everyone is pulling toward, to talk about what changes have been made, how those changes fit into the big picture and how important it is to have information quickly. This is not, of course, the time to use scare tactics or imply that people can be let go. Instead, highlight the carrot: point out the more interesting projects that can be accomplished by accountants who are no longer chasing transactions.

Identify one person to pull together information each month, including a list of all the entries made after the end of the month. List the source of the entry, either a person or a system, a short description of the entry, and the dollar amount. Leave a big space for notes after each entry. The designated person should count the number of items and keep a trend chart, updated each month with the number of entries. Be careful not to immediately label activities on this chart as value-added or non-value-added. It can be demeaning to a team member to hear an entry is non-value added. Instead, let the person who made the entry be the one to identify its value. Show that the target is to reduce the number of entries and the number of days it takes to close the books.

Now ask each team member to look over the list. Set parameters for what should be considered important, and then ask each person to target one error item, find out why it happened and how it can be corrected. To avoid conflict, team members should chose errors that spring from their own processes. Then each person can take an entry in her own sphere of responsibility and see if the process can be reduced by one day. Target the entries completed on the last day of close and try to reduce those by at least one day.

For even more excitement, try a breakthrough improvement. Here, we set aside time to focus on reducing the days it takes to do the job by half or more. For instance, Lantech found that one of the longest items was inventory obsolescence. Before becoming lean, inventory obsolescence was a significant expense and accounting calculated each element in the obsolescence reserve. In Lantech's case, the major elements were shipments by product line, write-offs from the obsolescence reserve, and the current level of inventory. For each item, a team looked to see when the data was available. For the longest item, they asked why it was so late and so on, until the team truly understood why it took so long to calculate the obsolescence reserve. Managers decided that the activity was not needed every month and could simply be checked twice a year because it changed in very small amounts. Next, a team found that the obsolescence expenses kept changing, largely because there were so many corrections for prior-month errors. Those errors were not recorded as obsolescence, but obviously should have been. At the same time, the team noticed that the correcting entries were very small and did not affect the total very much—at least not as a percentage of the total expenses. Also, the inventory number was not final until the fourth day.

The real breakthrough happened when the team realized they were trying to be precise in calculating a number that was completely unknown. An obsolescence reserve is just a guess at the dollar expense that will be incurred in future for inventory that is held today. This was the key to unlocking the mystery. Once the guesswork realization hit, Jean and her team decided to use the initial inventory number to calculate what the reserve should be in the future and use the amount of expenses from the general ledger to update the calculation. This turned out to be nearly the same number as it would have been, had they spent the time to book all the corrections and do the fine-tuning. Now, they use the same percentage each month to book the accrual and, at the end of the quarter, they review the reserve to see if it looks reasonable and check the percentage more formally. As Lantech became even leaner, producing only what the customers wanted, when it was wanted, obsolescence became a non-issue.

A company once asked Jean to look at the efforts they were making using kaizen techniques to reduce the complexity of the accounting activity. It was a complex operation because they not only did accounting for their organization but also for some of their distributors. There was lots of opportunity for improvement.

Leaders organized a kaizen and had team members map their current process. In looking over the process flow charts, Jean noticed that it took three days to calculate the bad debt reserve. The bad debt reserve has many of the same characteristics as the warranty reserve—it is a cost known only in the future, but must be recorded as an expense when the product is shipped out the door. Jean's antennae went up when she saw that it took three days to calculate a guess.

Jean discovered that it had not previously taken three days; in fact, it used to be very quick. But when auditors had reviewed the books, they suggested that the reserves were too low for the actual amount of bad debt activity. In accounting terms, it was not conservative enough. Still, the calculation took three days, which seemed excessive. To solve the problem of low reserves, the company had added some calculations to increase the reserve level—which, in their view, added sophistication to the calculation. In reality, they really just added complexity. The auditors did not say the reserve calculation was too simple, they just said the reserve wasn't enough. To illustrate this point, two mathematical calculations:

$$3 \times 4 = 12$$
$$(3 \times 10 \times 2) / 5 = 12$$

The second calculation is more complex but yields the same result. Three multiplied by four is 12. This calculation is no more complex but adds more quantity. Same thing as the bad debt experience. This company confused complexity for conservatism.

So here we are. You have eliminated most of the month-end transactions. Your systems are integrated; you can close books on a dime. The next big question is, do you need to close the books at all? This is not a question that can be answered glibly. But the question requires serious thought because it targets more closely the value of creating financial reports at all.

There are some very good reasons to close the books. Monthly financial statements help you keep tabs on whether plans are being met and allow you to monitor for any new information about where the business is moving. There may even be enough feedback for a celebration. Whatever the answer, it needs to fit your business. If you find the value of closing the books is small, perhaps running a daily financial is close enough. Maybe it only makes sense to close the books every quarter. The goal is to set aside the rules and traditions that no longer make sense and find what is right for your business.

8

BUDGETING AND CAPITAL PLANNING

IN MANY COMPANIES, BUDGET SEASON begins months in advance of the fiscal year's end and has all the trappings of a Senate confirmation. Executives use the process to jockey for position, to gauge status in the company and, in some cases, to actually get projects funded.

Meanwhile, the CFO dons the robes of a frantic St. Peter, seeming to judge the worthiness of all who pass before her even while scrambling to gather all possibly useful financial information and make it balanced and coherent. Capital requests fly in from all corners, each request padded against the arbitrary percentage cuts that people expect from accounting and upper management. A CFO can make enemies without even trying in budget season.

We could discuss budget reform here, but it is more useful to stop for a moment and ask, do we really need a budget at all?

The question may seem like heresy to those who know that the budget, along with the year-end closing of the books, is one of the major deliverables required of the accounting department each year. But if we are to get to the root of the accounting function, we must question our traditions and assumptions.

For some companies, the budget process provides structure to decision-making and an in-depth annual review. The trap that many companies fall into, however, is creating a single budget process that is followed year after year, whether each step is necessary for the current business objectives or not.

A few reasons—not all good—to create a budget:

1. To create common operating and financial assumptions for the coming year and to track results, allowing leaders to quickly respond and re-plan if the results veer off track

2. To provide a forum for selecting high-impact projects, and deselecting those which are not

3. To give management a benchmark in compensation issues

4. To meet possible lender requirement, and can ensure the business remains within the bank's covenants

5. To provide a shorthand method for communicating what decisions have been made: where new people will be added, how much advertising to do, pricing for a new product, etc.

6. To allow management to assess whether a growth plan outstrips the organization's ability to generate cash, particularly in low-profit margin businesses

7. To focus the organization on specific objectives, such as increasing the profit margin or increasing revenue growth, or improving customer communication

At its best and most useful, a budget is a common illustration of the business—its goals, realities and landmarks—that everyone can refer to during the year, to check the status of individual units against overall assumptions and targets. A budget can be especially important in organizations that are large and far-flung, where leaders don't check in with each other consistently. As the year goes on, individuals within any organization confront unique problems and make decisions independent of the group. A budget can offer those managers a landmark on the horizon to ensure they remain on the same path as the rest of the company. A budget can also offer a quick big picture. Once all the columns are in place, it's usually easy to see if all those start-up projects will make the company cash poor by the second quarter.

Bad reasons to keep a budget include tradition—otherwise known as a being in a rut—and creating something only to report against in the financial statements. Executives who create budgets solely to satisfy a top-down budget mandate eventually find themselves confronting numbers without reason. Those companies that tie personal compensation of executives to the budget set up a sometimes-destructive tension, where managers make decisions based on personal instead of business motivations.

"I don't think budgets are worth a hill of beans, personally," says Cold Spring Granite's CFO, Greg Flint. "They're based on guesswork and politics. Every year, you see financial guys negotiating for a tough budget and operations guys negotiating for an easy budget so they can look good. In the end, the financial guys own the budget. Operations can say, 'It's not my fault. You gave me a bad budget.' So, we got rid of budgets.

"What we do now is benchmark against this month last year and tell every department they must improve. If sales brought in $1 million last July with five people on staff, for instance, we might expect them to bring in $1.1 million this year with the same five people. Their goals are purely based on improvement, and we do not insist on arbitrary percentages for improvement."

When evaluating *if* and what type of budget an organization might need, one of the most useful tools for executives is the Five Whys. The name is partly intuitive, but the Five Whys does not stop with the fifth iteration of *why?* Instead, the Five Whys indicate a team's continued search for hidden facts and the true answer. As the team drills down into the true purpose of the budget—for that organization, for that year—new answers will become clear.

If the real reason for a budget is to get everyone on the same page, then the budget process needs to include plenty of time for team meetings and consensus building. If the budget is for the bank alone, on the other hand, there is little reason to spend significant time and resources creating the document. A smart CFO probably begins this process by asking bank officers what key elements they need from a budget—cash flow for example—and then focuses on obtaining this information.

"There is the one budget that we do, and it's for the bank," Greg Flint concedes. "I spend about 15 minutes creating it because the bankers don't really care about the budget, either. What they care about is whether we're going to break covenants."

The answers will not be the same from one company to the next, so there are few absolutes except this one: If the reason for a budget is "Because we have to" or "Because we always have," there is more work ahead for the team. At the end of the road, past the Five Whys and some serious soul-searching, however, the organization will be rewarded with a truly lean budget.

> **Lean Budget (v.):** the process of collecting and reflecting the economic results of a company's planned activities, focusing on the most relevant information in order to aid timely and accurate planning and decision-making.

Given the energy that has gone into defining whether a business needs a budget, and then what sort of budget might be of value, the intrinsic value of the chosen budget should be obvious. What might not be immediately obvious is the value of the budget process itself.

When budget creation is a process undertaken as an entire company, everyone understands what resources will be available and why. In a lean organization, this becomes part of the *hoshin*[7] *process* or policy deployment. If the company begins the budget cycle with the expected sales level for the coming year and concentrates on finding the resources to support it with an acceptable profit margin, for instance, the budget is not a dictator but a logical progression of a single goal. And then, with collaboration on the project, there will almost certainly be cross-germination of ideas within the company.

---

[7] Hoshin Kanri, part of the Toyota Production System, is a process of selecting—and deselecting—major projects to meet company goals and assigning personal responsibility.

With that goal in mind then, let's look to the journey. Particularly for companies that seek to increase understanding and communication, the budget process should be carefully considered and, above all, inclusive. The CFO—or any manager empowered to initiate the budget talks—should explore a variety of alternatives with a broad cross-section of people. With people talking to each other and challenging each other's ideas, we are lead to better choices.

Think back on the budget experiences you have participated in; consider what worked and what did not. Were the hours spent trying to get a column of numbers to add up to the "correct" amount worthwhile? Or was the discussion of how to achieve your number one project without adding more people to the staff more valuable? Was it better to figure out where to cut costs to make it believable to accounting, or was it looking at which markets had increased sales opportunity for your products? Looked at this way, it is easy to see that the budget itself is probably far less important than the journey everyone took to get there.

Lantech begins the budget process by defining a specific business objective and then—often, but not always—the leadership breaks part or all of the company into small idea-generating teams. One year, when creating new revenue was the top business objective, the first step in the budget was asking the entire company to form small teams and develop revenue-generating ideas. Another time, productivity was the goal and so that was the assigned subject for the teams. Another year small teams were asked to focus on a variety of assigned subjects, such as kaizen project management, new product ideas, cost elimination and medical benefits costs. Kaizen techniques are used for brainstorming, and team diversity is strongly encouraged to get fresh eyes on the subject, as well as experience.

Leading all of this in most companies will be the CFO, or someone else within the finance arena. Someone from accounting usually schedules the meetings, defines the information required and then compiles the data from each department or area for leadership to review. And it is usually accounting managers who critique and correct every manager's numbers, pointing out all the problems: numbers too high, too low, not consistent, not justified. No wonder some people hide when they see accountants coming.

Let's face it, budgeting and working the numbers is not the strong suit of many managers. Yet, every year we put them in the position of figuring it out for themselves while we wait in judgment, instead of offering help.

Rather than waiting until the end to provide an evaluation, begin with the planning process and assign one person from accounting to work with each of the various managers. Most accountants are good with spreadsheets, organizing, and doing simple math—skills that will be much valued by managers slogging through the numbers.

IDENTIFY AND COMMUNICATE GOALS WITH A LEAN BUDGET

Let's say that increasing profits is your company's goal because you need better profit margins to fund future investments or grow the business. One way to increase profits is to increase expenses at half the rate of sales. Give that goal to the teams and ask, "How would you do this?"

▶

If your company is organized by function or by product line, assign an assistant from accounting to each area within the established framework. In a larger company, specialists or financial analysts might fill this function. But a smaller company can achieve the same effect through thoughtful assignments: Perhaps the accountant who works with credit and collections or invoicing can work with the sales team while the accountants payable clerk works with the operations team. It might not be a perfect match every time, but no matter the match, the accounting specialist can be there to help organize information, get answers to questions and organize data into requested formats.

The specialist should be able to easily answer or research questions that vex managers, such as how much should be planned for relocating a person? How much can we expect telephone costs to rise next year? These specialists can, in turn, help to explain to the CFO or budget manager what the data means, or how the inconsistencies came to be and help move toward resolution.

One technique to use during lean budgeting that easily communicates the goal to everyone is to set an expense growth target at less than the sales growth target. For instance, if sales has identified that they think there is a 10 percent increase in sales for the next year, target increasing the expense rate at only five percent. If you have already created the Plain English Financials from Chapter 5, then focus on the natural expenses—as opposed to the variances or other fancy ways to express plain numbers—that can be influenced or changed.

▶

In too many organizations, people get so caught up forecasting telecommunications bills, month-by-month, department-by-department, that they miss the big picture and the opportunities. Changing this paradigm involves a careful look at the available staff and their assignments. Make sure that your best big-picture thinkers are not breaking down utilities bills.

Look at it this way: A budget process is like an accordion, always pulling open to include more points-of-view, then moving together again as decisions are made. In the first position, the accordion is compact and pushed together as managers define and understand the top-level business objectives. The accordion then expands to get wider input on possible strategies that could be used to reach the objectives. Pushed together again, executives decide on the top five or so strategies for the company. Expand to create action plans and identify resources required to meet the targets for each strategy. Pushed together, the accounting team then does the hard work that will make the process pay off by assessing whether total revenues, costs and resources to meet those strategies will be

Accounting can make this easier for everyone if they distribute, at the beginning of the process, a pro-forma expense budget using a five percent growth rate. This is distributed with the message that it is a starting point, not a dictate. Operations then spends energy on finding creative options or productivity gains to achieve a maximum 5 percent spending increase. The goal is to provide useful data to the departments so they don't spend valuable time crunching numbers.

▶

commercially successful. Expand again to resolve the gaps and issues identified, and so forth. Each expansion and coming together will get tighter, resulting in a harmonious organization, which thoroughly understands the strategies and targets.

Be careful, however: Pull the accordion apart too far to include too much detail and an accounting department could easily find itself stretched too far. Remember, only five to ten line items are normally critical to a company's success.

For most companies, the largest expense items on the budget will be salaries and benefits, so it is only natural that most of the focus in a budget process falls on how many people are needed in each area. Not all staffing expenses can be planned, however. Every year, a very significant impact to the actual spending is due to people voluntarily or involuntarily leaving their jobs. When there are job openings no salary is being paid, but that little windfall probably isn't in the budget either. Nor is the search for a new employee or the sudden need for six new clerks in customer service. There are three options for accounting:

Many lean manufacturers have identified a target of a one percent improvement per month. Instead of having this as a free-floating goal, this can be integrated into the budget process. Identify the resources currently required to do the work, then reduce that requirement by one percent a month in each category and apply that rate to your new sales level. That relationship will show you the resources needed to produce the new level of production, based on sales, including a 1 percent improvement per month.

1) Spend time in the budget process trying to guess who will leave when (otherwise known as the crystal ball tactic)

2) Ignore that personnel levels will change and budget for a fully staffed year, using any savings gleaned from staff shortages as a budget buffer

3) Look at the historical performance for attrition overall and budget that factor

Option 3 eliminates the waste and emotion of the guessing game that is implicit in option 1 and frees up funding sitting idle in option 2.

To use option 3: If the overall attrition and related gap in salary spending is two percent in the personnel budget, just reduce every personnel-spending budget by two percent. Not only is this quick and easy, it is usually more accurate. It won't be precise, but this is one of those instances when accuracy is more valuable than precision.

Most organization staffing is based on demand for the products, plus the current understanding of how many people it takes to make that product. This is certainly true for shop floor manufacturing, and is probably also true for staffing levels in Receiving, Shipping, Engineering, Spare Parts, Support and all other departments. So, a common estimate of demand, called *takt time* in lean organizations, is one of the first steps in the budget process. The demand may be expressed in dollars or units; it may be organized by work cell or product line or by category. What's most important is that product demand volume becomes the driver for staffing levels.

Demand should be the starting point for calculating the number of people needed in each area throughout the year. To demand, add the productivity factor expected to be achieved from kaizen or other improvement efforts. If a 1-percent per-month productivity increase is expected, each area can calculate what the resource needs will be, compared to the demand for the products.

> **Remember:**
> 1. Let the demand rate for your product drive your organization.
> 2. Combine your productivity goal with demand when determining staffing.

For the truly lean organization, staffing questions present new challenges throughout the year, not just at budget time. For those businesses that have worked hard to get double-digit productivity gains and have made the commitment not to lay off any employees made redundant during improvement work—an essential promise that a lean organization makes to its employees—there may be the question of extra people. Shop-floor associates, customer service representatives, and even accounting clerks can find themselves no longer needed in their former job functions. From a practical and a budget perspective, what do you do with those people?

Most companies quickly implement one of two choices: assignment to other positions in the company, opened by attrition, or into a labor pool. Typically, the labor pool becomes a constantly shifting team that concentrates on assisting further kaizen efforts. For instance, the labor pool might be directed to do follow-up work from an improvement team's kaizen week while waiting for new assignments. Other freed workers—skilled machinists, for instance—might form a machine build group, creating the smaller more versatile machines that lean manufacturers embrace. A cross-functional team might be put to work on developing new products or services. These are all valuable employees now, having been trained in lean concepts and having seen the process at work firsthand, and should be employed while waiting for new positions.

What's important here, from an accounting and budgeting point of view, is where these employees appear on financial statements. If the freed workers' salaries are still charged to the departments where they used to work, be aware that you will be undermining your improvement efforts. If a department makes process improvements that removes workers, but is still charged for the workers' salaries, there will be little financial incentive to continue looking for improvements. Instead, create a new cost center specifically for your labor pool and celebrate every time the salaries in that account take a leap upwards—that number represents improvements being made in the business.

It also gives the company a very visible sign of where associates are being freed and how many are in the pool. As new or replacement jobs open up, these are the first resources available for the job. Simultaneously, you may also have a Kaizen Promotion Office (KPO). This is the team hired specifically, or promoted from within, to run your kaizen or continuous improvement (C.I.) efforts. It is better to keep these two budgets—labor pool and KPO—separate or your KPO expenses can seem to run out of control. The KPO might direct the efforts of the labor pool, but it is usually a mistake to actually attach transitional workers to that office. Instead, keep the resource pool separate and that way, when a job needs to be filled and an associate can be plucked from the pool, you will be getting a job filled for free.

Just as personnel issues are viewed differently in a lean environment, so are new capital requests. For decades, accounting courses have been churning out students who know exactly how to evaluate capital requests—the wrong way.

The most important thing a CFO can do for a company is to constantly keep the big picture—the entire value chain, from raw material supplier to distributor—in mind. When evaluating capital expense requests, this means considering the needs of the process as well as the bottom line. For instance, in years past, accountants might consider three new widget makers when a new one was needed. The machine that put out the widget fastest was often considered the best deal. Even if the machine were a few thousand dollars more, so long as it ran 20 hours a day putting out thousands of widgets, it would be worth the investment. You don't need thousands of that type of widget? Well put it in stock, against a rainy day.

CFOs in lean environments now realize that the smaller, more flexible machine is actually needed. Perhaps the perceived per-widget cost is fractionally higher, but resources are not being wasted in the production and storage of useless widgets. And when the market changes its mind about the size and color next month, businesses want versatile machines that can adapt along with the company's needs.

When considering new capital expenses, the questions to be asked are:

- ❑ Will it reduce inventory?
- ❑ How much will it delay cost?
- ❑ Is it flexible? Will it easily accommodate product changes?
- ❑ Can we use a smaller, single-purpose machine—maybe one designed and built internally?
- ❑ Will it help us avoid inventory, especially the inventory that clogs up the flow between processes?
- ❑ Does it help us meet takt time?

Smart companies no longer justify buying large equipment based on a lower per-part cost if that part must be run in big batches to achieve the savings. Excess inventory, lean executives know, clogs up communication between value chain partners—do you know if your current supplier can really deliver to your new growth expectations?—and makes responsiveness sluggish. Batch manufacturing creates costs and waste that accounting must be vigilant against, particularly while reviewing capital requests. If a cost benefit analysis is performed, the cost should be net cost: the cost of the project less any permanent inventory reductions that it will achieve. This allows for projects that trade one type of investment—inventory—for another type—capital equipment—but achieve increased capacity and flexibility to meet changing customer demands. In fact, if the permanent inventory reduction is equal to or greater than the capital investment, the project generates an immediate benefit and is self-funding.

A capital plan typically focuses on the plant, property and equipment a company expects to need to meet the business plan. However, accounts receivable, inventory and other working capital are large users of cash and funding. Rarely do companies have top-level improvement targets here. But in a lean organization, inventory level or turns will be a key metric of success.

Accounts receivable days outstanding can also be improved by paying close attention to customers' compliance with sales terms. The capital savings can be fundamental to a company's ability to grow. In the next chapter, you will see how this capital can really drive shareholder and enterprise value.

9

LEAN ACQUISITIONS

IT IS OFTEN SAID THAT COMPANIES THAT ARE NOT growing are shrinking. There is no such thing as standing still. The company that adopts lean business strategies, that allows a culture of continuous improvement to take root in its processes and people, always ends up in a better position to grow. And lean organizations that choose to supplement growth by purchasing other companies will find they have advantages they never imagined in the competitive world of mergers and acquisitions.

Consider the case of Wiremold. In less than two years, a lot of hard work improving processes and reducing inventory freed up over $11 million in cash (see Figure 9.1). This reduction in inventory must be viewed as a key element of the lean strategy and not just a better inventory management system. For Wiremold, the cash from that liquidated inventory financed the first five acquisitions in the second year.

1993 inventory at 1990 turnover rate	16.7 million
Actual 1993 inventory	5.6 million
Cash flow savings	11.2 million
Cost of first 5 1993 acquisitions	10.0 million
Cycle time reductions = $24 million in new sales	

Figure 9.1 Inventory Reductions Finance Growth

Keep this in mind as you consider inventory: If it is assumed that the carrying cost of inventory is 10 percent (most MRP systems assume twice this amount), then income has been enhanced by $1.1 million through inventory reduction. The five companies Wiremold acquired during the second year of lean, at a combined purchase price of $10 million, had total sales of $24 million and an average operating income of 10 percent, or $2.4 million. Therefore, converting cash from financing inventory to financing growth increased income by $3.5 million. For privately owned companies with limited access to capital this enables them to internally finance accelerated growth.

Companies that apply lean lessons to the realm of acquisitions will find significant benefits, namely:

1. Lean philosophies provide everyone with a clear game plan as teams confront the merging of another company with their own
2. Excess assets in the target company, such as inventory and space, are quickly freed up
3. Risk is reduced by lowering the net cost of an acquisition and reducing the payback period

For Lantech, the same renewed focus on growth evolved over time. With the success of lean in product development, manufacturing, engineering, sales and accounting, profits and market share were dramatically increased. Proud and confident in these skills, Lantech had a thirst for more; it has continued to invest in new products and new markets. Improved profits and reduced inventory levels also meant the balance sheet showed cash strength and funds to invest. With its lean experience, Lantech leadership also knew similar results could be achieved at other companies and kept that in mind when considering acquisition targets.

The biggest advantage a lean executive has in the marketplace is that he has learned to look at companies differently.

Look at the key operating information that illustrates an acquisition target in Figure 9.2. This manufacturing company has slow growth and is not particularly well managed. We see low productivity, $70,000 in sales per employee, and a four-percent operating income. It is typical of most batch-and-queue companies, in terms of inventory management practices, with just 2.4 annual inventory turns. In the three years prior to acquisition, gross profit has remained flat at 25 percent, indicating no significant operational improvement. Although the target company's operating income has increased as a percentage of sales,

¥ Sales: $160m	¥ Head count: 2,300
¥ Gross Profit: $40m (25%)	¥ Sales/employees: $70k
¥ Operating Profit: $6m (4%)	¥ Purchase Price: $80m
¥ Inventory: $50m	¥ Sales Growth: 3-5%
¥ Space: 1m square feet	

Figure 9.2 Acquisition Example

this has been done through aggressive cost reductions in non-manufacturing functions—sales, general and administrative—and slashed budgets for product development and training.

The purchase price is high for this company, at 13.3 times the operating income, but the products it manufactures and sells are strategic to the buyer. It is worth a significant premium, the buyer decides, to keep this fish out of the jaws of the buyer's competitors. Let's say for a moment that the interested buyer was a typical batch-and-queue operator. His analysis of the target would probably look like Figure 9.3. We accept that the target company's market is mature, so sales are projected to continue to grow at the historical rate of four percent.

	Pre-Acquisition			êPost-Acquisition				
	Base -2	Base -1	Base Year	Base +1	Base +2	Base +3	Base +4	Base +5
Sales	147	153	160	166	173	180	187	195
Gross Profit	37	38	40	42	45	48	51	54
Gross Profit %	25.0%	25.0%	25.0%	25.5%	26.0%	26.5%	27.0%	27.5%
Operating Income	4	5	6	8	10	11	12	14
Operating Income %	3.0%	3.0%	4.0%	4.5%	6.0%	6.3%	6.6%	7.0%
Inventory	46	48	50	46	43	40	38	36
Inventory Turns	2.4x	2.4x	2.4x	2.7x	3.0x	3.3x	3.5x	3.8x
Sales/Employee	70k	70k	70k	75k	78k	81k	84k	88k

Figure 9.3 A Traditional View of a Target Company

The buyer believes he can improve productivity by almost five percent per year and more than double operating income over a five-year period. He also believes he can improve inventory turns at the target company by 50 percent over that same period.

Working with these assumptions, Figure 9.4 then shows that operating income in the early years will only be sufficient to pay interest and minimal principal payments on the acquisition debt. At the end of five years, only $30.4 million of the $80 million has been paid down. If the economy were to enter into a downturn after five years—no small risk—servicing the acquisition debt could become difficult and represents a potential risk to the buyer. Most acquisition models do not assume economic downturns and therefore generally present the best-case scenario. Recession risk is generally ignored.

Year	Operating Income	Interest Expenses	Income Before Taxes	Income Taxes	Net Income	Inventory Decrease	Cash From Operations	Principal Balance	Total Debt Service
Beginning Year 1	8	6.4	1.6	0.6	1.0	4.0	5.0	- 80.0	11.4
End Yr 2	10	6.0	4.0	1.6	2.4	3.0	5.4	69.6	11.4
End Yr 3	11	5.6	5.4	2.2	3.2	3.0	6.2	63.4	11.8
End Yr 4	12	5.0	7.0	2.8	4.2	2.0	6.2	57.2	11.2
End Yr 5	14	4.6	9.4	3.8	5.6	2.0	7.6	49.6	12.2
End Yr 6	16	4.0	12.0	4.8	7.2	2.0	9.2	40.2	13.2
End Yr 7	18	3.2	14.8	5.9	8.9	2.0	10.9	29.3	14.1
End Yr 8	20	2.3	17.7	7.1	10.6	2.0	12.6	16.7	14.9
End Yr 9	22	1.3	20.7	8.3	12.4	2.0	14.4	2.3	15.7
End Yr 10	24	0.2	23.8	9.5	14.3	2.0	16.3	0	2.5
								-	118.4

Note: Assumes that spending for new capital equipment equals depreciation, creating a net zero cash-flow effect

Figure 9.4 Traditional Assumptions: Debt Service Analysis

Now let's step into the head of a lean practitioner who is considering the same target. His analysis looks like Figure 9.5. Experience has shown us that by the second year, sales growth can be accelerated due to better customer service and aggressive new product development. That same product development also shows better profits now, due to the employment of lean strategies. This is possible even in companies that are in mature markets.

This example, which is based firmly on the authors' experience, shows sales growth is assumed to accelerate at the rate of seven percent for the second year and 10 percent per year for the following years. Productivity gains of 20 percent per year are achievable and inventory turns will improve 15 times by year five. As a result, operating income can be improved to

12 percent, versus 7 percent in the traditional mindset. As demonstrated in Figure 9.5, all of the acquisition debt can be paid off by the end of the fifth year when the buyer knows lean.

The buyer who comes from a lean environment knows these results are possible because he can spot the waste in a batch and queue environment and knows how to use kaizen to turn waste into positive dollars. Most importantly, he knows that the transformation begins on day one.

	Pre-Acquisition			ÊPost-Acquisition				
Sales	Base -2 147	Base -1 153	Base Year 160	Base +1 166	Base +2 178	Base +3 195	Base +4 215	Base +5 237
Gross Profit	37	38	40	45	52	62	73	83
Gross Profit %	25.0%	25.0%	25.0%	27%	29%	32%	34%	35%
Operating Income	4	5	6	10	13	17	22	23
Operating Income %	3.0%	3.0%	4.0%	6.0%	7.5%	8.5%	10.0%	12.0%
Inventory	46	48	50	30	18	13	11	10
Inventory Turns	2.4x	2.4x	2.4x	4.0x	7.0x	10.0x	13.5x	15.0x
Sales/Employee	70k	70k	70k	85k	100k	122k	147k	170k

Figure 9.5 The Analysis of a Lean Practitioner

If an acquired company is allowed to continue to operate in its historical manner for months after the acquisition, however, implementing lean will be more difficult. On the first day, everyone must be informed of the acquirer's lean strategy. Widespread education and training must begin immediately. There must be an immediate recognition by the acquired company's employees that the historical method of operating has ended and that a new way of thinking has taken center stage. When this happens, significant gains begin to occur almost immediately and a momentum quickly builds toward general acceptance—and even an embrace—of continuous improvement.

A comparison of the key metrics of these two models shows that at the end of five years, the lean company has:

- ❏ No debt vs. almost $50 million
- ❏ 10 percent growth rate vs. 4 percent
- ❏ 65 percent more operating income
- ❏ 37 percent less people
- ❏ 75 percent less inventory
- ❏ 55 percent less interest cost

The lean company has also most likely cut its space utilization in half and improved customer service. If the economy were to enter into a downturn at this point, the company is in a much better condition to weather the storm than in the traditional mode.

Please note: This analysis does not address the academic issues of whether maintaining some level of debt leverage is good, but simply looks at the issue of reducing the risk involved in an acquisition by reducing the payback period.

Or, look at it in a simpler way: If we consider the total cost of the acquisition to be the entire debt service—principal plus interest, which is assumed to be 8 percent in this case—then the cost of the acquisition has been reduced by $21.1 million if a lean strategy is employed. Using this knowledge, a company can afford to pay a higher premium in a bidding situation and take strategic acquisitions away from the competition.

In figures 9.6, 9.7 and 9.8, we have included some actual before and after results achieved by applying lean strategies to several acquisitions. The approach used in each company was identical.

On the first day after the acquisition was complete, the buyer held a meeting with all employees (each was a single location company) and introduced the employees to the company's lean strategy. Using lean teachers pulled from other operations, the buyer then began an intensive education in lean and kaizen within the first two weeks.

Year	Operating Income	Interest Expenses	Income Before Taxes	Income Taxes	Net Income	Inventory Decrease	Cash From Operations	Principal Balance	Total Debt Service
Beginning Year 1	10	6.4	3.6	1.4	2.2	20.0	22.2	- 80.0	28.6
End Yr 2	13	4.6	8.4	3.4	5.0	12.0	17.0	40.8	21.6
End Yr 3	17	3.3	13.7	5.5	8.2	5.0	13.2	27.6	16.5
End Yr 4	22	2.2	19.8	7.9	11.9	2.0	13.9	13.7	16.1
End Yr 5	23	1.1	21.9	8.8	13.1	1.0	14.1	0	14.8
								-	97.6
Note: Assumes that spending for new capital equipment equals depreciation, creating a net zero cash-flow effect									

Figure 9.6 Lean Assumptions: Debt Service Analysis

In the case of company "A" shown in Figure 9.6, the initial education was accomplished that first morning and kaizen events began that first afternoon. By the end of day one, a long conveyor belt assembly line was dissembled and hauled out to the parking lot. This represented a significant emotional event in the lives of those employees and sent a clear message that everyone was working under a different operating philosophy. As is readily apparent from this example, significant gains can be achieved in a short time when the lean strategy is rigorously applied from the outset.

Figure 9.7 represents an acquired company that was the market-share leader in its product category. Upon acquisition, lean principles were applied to the company's new product development process—getting the voice of the customer and creating cross-functional teams to ensure a profitable and workable

Acquisition A			
	1997	1998	% Change
Sales	100%	40%	-60%
Inventory	100%	50%	-50%
Head Count	88	55	-38%
Operating Profit	-5%	14%	

Figure 9.7 An Acquisition Sample

product—with great results. In spite of its previous market share position, sales were increased by 133 percent within three years. The company did this by developing new products that grew the market, while at the same time increasing its market-share position with more user-friendly products. Significant operating improvements were achieved in both productivity and asset management, making it the low-cost producer.

Acquisition C			
	Year 1	Year 5	% Change
Sales	$14.8 million	$23.3.million	+57%
Operating Income	-$0.7 million	$4.8 million	
Sales/Employee	$98K	$167K	+70%
Inventory Turns	4.1x	27.9x	+580%

Figure 9.8 Acquisition C

The company in Figure 9.8 had aggressively pursued a Total Quality Management program prior to being acquired. However, it was in a very competitive market and was trying to compete with products from foreign low-cost producers. The TQM activities enabled the company to achieve some gains, but not enough to be profitable.

By applying lean principles, the business quickly improved its productivity, became profitable and, by emphasizing custom products that required short lead times, was able to grow at a rapid pace in spite of low-cost foreign competitors. Its ability to compete on the basis of time gave it opportunities that the long lead-time batch competitors could not match, regardless of price.

In each of these cases, the application of lean principles as a business strategy—not just an inventory management program—allowed the lean acquirer to gain significant competitive advantage. In those cases where the acquirer was competing with other companies to buy the target company, it was able to offer a premium and win the target. In spite of this, in each case the purchase price paid was recovered in less than five years.

10

THE ROAD AHEAD

THERE IS A CHINESE PROVERB THAT SAYS, "In doing anything, the first step is the most difficult." We have found that the second step is also tricky and important, as is the third; and the order in which the steps are taken can be critical. Because we are talking about such fundamental change to an organization, we are often asked for a roadmap or step-by-step guide to a transformation to lean management accounting. Of course, there is no simple answer.

There are pivotal and universal steps that need to be taken, however, and a loose order in which most businesses will want to take those steps. The first and most important action is that all senior leaders must adopt lean as a business strategy and not a manufacturing tactic. The CEO, the CFO, and the rest of the management team must be committed to focusing on and transforming any aspect of the business that does not support that strategy.

A lean transformation often represents a significant shift in a company's culture and the CEO needs to be personally involved in change management. Virtually every business publication has published numerous articles discussing the subject of changing corporate cultures, but few have described culture in any detail. In its simplest form, a company is comprised of a group of individuals that hold some common values and beliefs. Those values and beliefs cause them to behave in a certain way, and when they get the results they expect and desire from those behaviors, their values and beliefs are reinforced. This self-reinforcing cycle represents culture.

In order to change a culture, we must somehow break the current cycle. Although a CEO may make statements about adopting a new set of value and beliefs (e.g. "We're going to become customer focused.") this rarely changes culture because people usually continue to act and react in their same patterns. We are creatures of habit. Therefore, in order to change culture, there must be some intervention that will force people to behave differently. Once they do, and begin to experience different and better results, their values and beliefs will begin to evolve and a new culture will take hold. Figure 10-1 illustrates this principle.

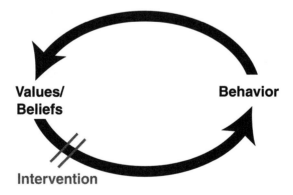

Figure 10.1 Intervention is Required to Break Patterns of Behavior

To create new behaviors, the first and most important action we can take is to begin immediately. Don't establish a task force to spend six months studying lean and come up with a traditional economic (e.g. ROI) justification for it. Our strong recommendation is, simply, this: Lean works, so just accept it and get started.

The second action is to create a clear statement about lean becoming the company's business strategy and distribute it throughout the company. Repeat the message any way you can. Everything the company does must be measured against this strategy statement, so it needs to be clear and concise.

Third action: get help. As previously discussed, the principles of lean are easy to agree with but hard to implement and sustain. There are several sources of good help and one of them should be chosen.

Next, the CEO must begin to act in a way that requires others to change their behavior. Of the many things that need to be done, some of them are:

- ❑ Provide lean education to all management and supervisory personnel early in the process. Ensure that all leaders become ordinary team members on a kaizen event and develop plans to bring lean principles into their own functional areas.
- ❑ Provide "air cover" for early adopters. Don't let naysayers get in the way.
- ❑ Flatten the organization and re-organize into product family-based operational teams.
- ❑ Provide an environment where it is acceptable to fail. When people try something new and it doesn't work, they should not be penalized.

❏ Change the management incentive compensation system to include customer service and working capital objectives and to eliminate individual objectives.

❏ Hold weekly meetings with the CEO and senior management where product team leaders report on where they stand on the new metrics (see Chapter 3). Reports should include improvement actions taken during the past week, improvement plans for the following week and a list of resources or support needed from management.

This last point is very important. By having product team leaders report every week on new metrics and process improvement efforts and successes, those leaders will quickly understand that achieving continuous improvement is now an important part of their job. These meetings go a long way in changing the company's culture. (At Wiremold, it wasn't until after year five of our lean transformation that the meetings were cut down to every other week.)

Beginning a lean initiative in the accounting department requires a few additional actions. Before we begin that discussion, however, it is important to emphasize one of the most important principles: integration. All accounting professionals must participate in all the education received by operations personnel. This is a vital step toward integrating accounting with the business as a whole, as we have emphasized throughout this book. The financial staff must participate in at least two kaizen teams each during the first three months of a lean initiative. Every member of the accounting department should join one setup-reduction kaizen and one kaizen that creates a one-piece-flow cell. Do not let the accounting staff opt out of this important work, as these early months will establish tone and communicate your commitment. Besides, the staff will need a better understanding of the company's work in order to fulfill their expanding roles.

Both the financial staff and senior management will also need some education as to why the accounting processes, including the financial statements, must change. There will very likely be some reluctance to change; taking a course together will provide a forum for everyone to air his or her feelings and come to a common understanding.

Next, accounting staff should begin changing their business processes at a pace commensurate with the operational changes. If the business processes are changed too rapidly, that could create havoc in operations. If changed too slowly, accounting becomes a roadblock. See chapters 2 and 4 for detailed change plans and ideas for individual projects.

Plain English financial statements similar to that in Figure 6-2 should be created as soon as possible. Most companies will not be able to dismantle standard cost statements immediately, but the new format can be prepared in parallel, in spreadsheet format. As these statements are created, the CFO should distribute them as an alternative view to other senior leaders and ask for feedback. This will help accounting create the most useful financial statements for the business and get others accustomed to the new document.

The CFO should also take the lead in establishing a communications plan for each of the company's stakeholders. Everyone needs to understand the benefits of the lean transformation, and to appreciate both the immediate and long-term effects on their jobs and their working lives. The audiences and what they need to hear include:

Senior management: Subjects for discussion should include strategy, organization, performance measurement, financial statements, compensation formulas and the short-term negative financial impact caused by reducing inventories, among others. Much of this should be covered in the initial education courses, but continuing communication is vital to a profound shift in culture and business.

Board of Directors: This should include the same subjects covered with senior management. Because a board will not necessarily be available for education courses, however, consider creating and delivering a presentation.

Shareholders: They need to know what the strategy is, its benefits and the negative P&L effect of reducing inventories during the transition. In a privately owned company, communication can generally occur concurrent with the communication to the board of directors. In a publicly owned company, however, it is not practical to deliver this level of information to shareholders. Instead, you will want to concentrate on communication to the financial analysts that follow the company's stock. In this way, the analysts will be able to understand the company's operating results in light of the strategy and can discount the negative effects of inventory reductions. The company should also consider having analysts participate in kaizen events in order to learn firsthand the potential benefits of lean.

Employees: These stakeholders need to understand the benefits of lean and learn how they will contribute and profit. (The authors believe that profit sharing is the best way to bring the Productivity = Wealth principal down to the employee level.) Factory employees that have held a single-skilled job (e.g. punch press operator) must be gently and firmly told that in the future, they will be expected to become multi-skilled as manufacturing cells are put into place. Most importantly, everyone must be told—and told again—that no one will lose employment as a result of productivity gains.

Unions: Union management must be brought into the change process early. In addition to explaining the reasons for change, the benefits to the membership should also be explained. In most cases, there will be provisions in the union contract that do not support lean and need to be changed. Begin this dialogue early as well, while emphasizing the potential benefits.

Banks: If the company's loan agreements contain traditional financial covenants, a dialogue with the bank needs to begin because the company's balance sheet will begin to change. For example, if there is a covenant for working capital (typically 2:1), this will become an issue as the company dramatically reduces inventory. Short-term earnings penalties, due to inventory reduction, should be brought into the discussion here, as well. Covenants should be renegotiated to focus more on cash flow coverage rather than asset coverage. Be prepared to explain the benefits of change to the business.

Auditors: Audit plans are based on the business processes and controls that a company uses. If those processes normally change very little from year to year, audit plans tend to remain constant. Once a company embarks on a lean transformation, business processes will change rapidly. This will have an impact on audit plans and auditors need to have adequate time to revise those plans to reflect the new environment. Letting them discover the changes when they arrive to begin the audit will cause confusion and stress.

Suppliers: Although the transformation process begins within the company, eventually it will include suppliers. At some point, suppliers will be required to deliver smaller quantities more frequently, and will be expected to do so by becoming lean, not by carrying more inventory. Suppliers will most likely need to learn to work within the kanban replenishment system. Most lean companies also significantly reduce the number of suppliers used as they stop the old play-one-supplier-against-the-other game on pricing. Accordingly, suppliers need to understand the rules for surviving that process of elimination and the criteria upon which they will be judged. Encourage suppliers to participate in shop floor kaizens, especially in areas that use the products they supply, and to send critical personnel— not salespeople—to represent the company on a team.

Customers: Eventually, the benefits of lean need to be translated into benefits for the company's customers. If benefits are not felt at the customer level, the company has not fully capitalized on the competitive advantage of a lean strategy. At some point in the transformation process, customers need to become educated on the benefits of lean available to them and how they can take advantage.

There is much to do. As we all know by now, it is easy to talk about lean, but far more difficult to achieve real transformation. But *doing* is the key point. Talking about lean does not create a better-run business with less firefighting. Issuing a new vision statement does not create greater profit, using fewer resources.

In trying to change the company's culture, employees will respond to what management does more readily than what it says. As someone once said, "The tongues in our shoes speak

166

louder than the tongues in our mouths." Passively delegating the implementation of lean down the organization will send, quite loudly, the wrong message. Therefore, the most important step is for the CEO and CFO to become active leaders in the lean transformation.

11

THE PAYOFF

A DYNAMIC BUSINESS ENVIRONMENT where profit and personal fulfillment can flourish is everyone's goal. We have been able to satisfy these goals by creating lean businesses. This is not to say that we have discovered all the answers. But here is what we have found: benefit for all the stakeholders in a business, from customers to employees, business partners and shareholders.

The Wiremold Company had about $100 million in revenue and was worth about $30 million at the beginning of its lean journey. About ten years later, in the year 2000, it had $430 million in revenues. During this period, it increased its base business significantly through aggressive new product development and made 21 acquisitions. In the year 2000 it was sold for $770 million. In a decade of tremendous economic growth at the close of the twentieth century, this manufacturer had out-performed the S&P 500 by more than double.

Lantech, as a privately held company that has had no ownership change, does not have confirmable market values to compare for this decade. However, there are some simple indicators of the success derived from lean. From 1990 to 2000, sales increased 80 percent with the same number of employees. As a result, Lantech moved from an unprofitable position to the top third profit category of the market segment, as measured by the Fortune 500.

The minimization of working capital and superior profit has created access to large funds to fuel product expansion. So far, Lantech has acquired companies with complimentary products in the U.S. and Holland, enhancing the company's offerings. During the manufacturing sector recession of 2001, the financial strength accumulated over time allowed Lantech to maintain profitability despite a 20 percent decline in demand, buy the two new companies, and launch a 100 percent surge in new product development efforts. So, by consistently improving the strength of Lantech over 10 years, the company was able not only to avoid the severe impact associated with an economic downturn, but also to capitalize on it.

The question is, with these metrics, why doesn't everyone go lean? The sad fact is, many companies begin the journey only to be derailed after a few improvements on the front lines. Those companies that stumble and fall do so because they fail to see that lean is a business strategy. When lean is not integrated across the entire company, conflicting business practices will inhibit lean. When accounting is kept in the dark, it will not have the tools to disclose the correct impact of the lean effort.

Lean is not a flavor-of-the-month improvement process for manufacturing or customer service. It is not an inventory management system. Taken holistically, lean is a business strategy that has colored the way we operate throughout our value chains—from supplier to distributor, from shop floor to executive strategy sessions. To keep lean out of the business office is to deny the company its full potential for success.

Some enlightened banks now look to lean companies as their best investment opportunities—but only when the CFO is completely on board.

"Because [lean companies] don't carry a heavy inventory and receivables burden, they are focusing on generating maximum cash flow to finance growth, and not to just look to the bank to borrow the most they can. It demonstrates to us that they are focusing on the right things," says William H. Morgan, Executive Vice President of Fleet Boston Financial.

When the CFO is paying attention to all aspects of the business—growth, margins and asset management—Fleet Boston sees a better customer. But the inverse is also true.

"If the CFO can't explain the company's strategy and how it impacts on operations, marketing, etc. then that forces us to bypass him and deal directly with the CEO. Just knowing the numbers isn't enough," Mr. Morgan says. In other words, financial executives who ignore lean deny themselves the potential to become true partners.

Yet, there are still accountants out there who seem to believe that "road blocker" is in the job description. Through fear or ignorance, they cling to the idea of the black art of numbers and impenetrable variances—as if their existence depended on the ability to complicate and confuse.

"CFOs must stop protecting their turf and get out of the 'You can't do that' mindset," cautions Art Byrne, now-retired CEO of The Wiremold Company and one of the earliest adopters of lean in the U.S.

"In many cases, operating people understand the benefits of changing to lean but can't move forward because of the financial organization and how it establishes performance measurements. But if the CFO has a good business perspective and takes the time to understand the real economic benefits of lean, he can become an advocate of change and adjust the company's accounting and measurements systems in order to help everyone in the company implement the lean strategy, " Byrne says.

In talking with CEOs, that idea of the chief financial officer as an advocate for change became a repeating theme. Those CFOs who advocated change, who cleared a path for transformation at the side of the CEO, were the most valued business partners.

"What I look for in a financial executive is a visionary with a controller's mindset," says TBM Consulting Group's CEO Anand Sharma. "Management performance reviews, I often say, is a game of chicken. We have people trying to present only the positive side in their numbers, hoping that nobody asks the tough questions. This leads to some very creative reporting because there are so many ways to dissect the facts. So, from the controller mindset, I expect dependable reliability. I need to know that what is being reported is consistently true; the controller brings realism and sense to the reports.

"Then from the visionary side, I want someone who has business sense, who has good judgment beyond the numbers. He or

172

she should be able to make the numbers more relevant for decision-making, and be able to reveal the impact of decisions on
cash flow and intangible improvements. He should be able to
look through the clouds and forecast the future—to see the
effect of lean in one, two or five years.

"The CFO should be a visionary partner of the CEO. His job
is not to create the transformation; it is to clear the way for the
CEO and to keep the wolves off his back.

"In a large company, he should be selling lean to the board
through his understanding of the numbers and the business
impact in the future. In a small company, he will also be the
controller so he will have to be reliable, solid as a rock and consistent. He or she must be able to provide an interpretation of
the long-term implications of lean when reporting to management. Those are the best CFOs to have—those who can explain
the short-term realities and long-term implications."

There is certainly a great need for financial leaders who can
partner with CEOs and provide the kind of support required in
tomorrow's quickening business environment. Where will these
leaders come from, and who will train them?

At this writing, a great shortage exists in the accounting field.
The number of accounting degrees awarded in 1998-1999 was
20 percent lower than in 1995-1996. In the second half of the
1990s, enrollment in accounting programs dropped by 22
percent. One of the reasons most often given for that stiff
drop-off in accounting enrollments is the fact that accounting
education has simply not kept pace with changes in business
practices.

So now accounting firms fight over qualified candidates or look to other countries to import those interested in a career in finance. Why are there so few people entering this field?

One reason for the low turnout might be the generally accepted perception of accountants as hapless bean counters. There are no TV shows featuring accountants in a positive light and we didn't make the cover of Time magazine until 2002, when some financial executives were shown in handcuffs. We are not suggesting that we need to be elevated to rock star status, but we know that we must capture the imaginations of young people in order to keep fresh ideas circulating.

To do this, universities must adapt the curriculums to be more dynamic and encompass a larger idea of the accountant as business partner. We want lean to be a topic of study, not only in the Operation Management courses, but also in Human Resources, Strategic Planning and Accounting. This will seed the newly graduating student with ideas that will make her more valuable to a business from day one.

But the schools can only go so far. It is up to us, the current leaders, to create environments open to change and new ideas, to make our work attractive to the best and brightest of the upcoming generation.

Recently, a young woman was talking with Jean about what she might study in college. This young woman seemed to have many of the characteristics required for success in accounting. Of course, Jean encouraged her, but in the back of her mind she worried that this young woman might go through all of that hard work and land in a company that was not dynamic, not

174

open and fun—not lean. Sure, there are financial executives vital to their companies' successes, who encourage fresh ideas and practices and remain flexible. But the perception of accounting as boring drudgery exists because, far too often, it is true.

From the chapters of this book, you may have gotten the impression that creating an accounting transformation is difficult, time-consuming work. It is. It will require all of your skills as a professional and a human being—including intelligence, creativity, compassion and vision—to do it well. It is not a journey with a destination, but a way of life.

A commercial banker who was once presented with a company's new lean approach responded with, "That sounds great. So when do you think you will be finished?" The answer, of course, is you will never be finished. Lean is a strategy, a discipline that permeates and changes the culture, the people, of a business.

This is not the end of the story. We fervently hope this book inspires others to try new techniques, to push the borders further, to go into unexplored areas of the business and become personally involved in kaizen or continuous improvement events. Shake up the financial statement.

Rediscover your relevance.

LEAN ACCOUNTING CONCEPTS & PRINCIPLES

1) Accuracy is more valuable than precision.

Accuracy and precision are often the same. An invoice of $200 is both accurate and precise. But when they are not the same, it will take more time and cost to be precise than to be accurate. Quick test: if a value were 10% higher, would you make a different decision? This test will help you decide how much precision is needed to be accurate.

2) Do not confuse a fixed cost for a variable cost.

Different decisions require different data. A variable cost is one that will change in correlation with volume. If you do not sell a widget, you will not need the material to produce the widget. That is a variable cost. If you do not sell a widget, you will still need to keep the lights on in the engineering department. That is a fixed cost. Look at the change in cash to help differentiate fixed from variable.

3) Eliminate absorption accounting for manufacturing transactions.

While labor and overhead manufacturing cost is required to be capitalized for unsold inventory by Generally Accepted Accounting Principles (GAAP), it is not required to absorb for every inventory transaction. It can be analytically created for all inventory by a product line or grouping. So, stop making hundreds of piece-part transactions. If you have stable WIP, or the lead time of the product is shorter than the fiscal period, transactional absorption adds no improved understanding of operational performance.

4) The next cost is more important than the last cost. Or, mind the whiplash.

Just because a machine will produce 1000 widgets at a lower cost per unit, does not mean producing 1000 widgets is the best decision. Perhaps a smaller machine that produces the quantity needed when it is needed will reduce your future costs more than the big machine. Also, as accountants, this principle can help us remember that putting focus on the future outcome of the business may be more productive than looking backward.

5) Accounting transactions are not the only source of information.

Data needed on the shop floor can be created there and remain on the shop floor. For example, units produced each day for a specific line can be tracked and utilized on that line. If it is not necessary for others to know, and is not needed in accounting reports, leave it out of the reporting system. Attendance data may not be needed in the accounting systems either.

6) Once and be done.

Rework is the most expensive work. This is true not only on the shop floor but especially so in the office. Take the time to enter original data (orders, specifications, drawings, etc.) correctly and ensure its accuracy before passing it on through the business process.

7) "Accounting said" is not a reason.

Frequently business processes are created to meet an "accounting need." Always ask the follow-up question in order to understand why a task needs to be performed and to know whether it will serve the company's needs.

8) Financial statements should be usable by non-accountants.

The purpose of financial statements is to aid managers in making decisions. One should not need an accounting degree to get that information.

9) You are what you measure.

Measurements affect behavior. Deciding which performance measures to use for your organization can mean the difference between real productivity gains and dysfunctional behavior.

10) Financial engineering will not yield productivity gains.

11) A dollar is more valuable in flexible capacity than in inventory.

12) In cost accounting, the less allocation the better.
Allocations, by their nature, involve choices between methods and estimates and are not actionable.

LIST OF FIGURES

INDEX